HOW TO RUN FACILITATED WORKSHOPS

A pragmatic guide to successful meetings

Kevin Barron

Contents

1

INTRODUCTION

I herded chickens once. I was staying on my aunt's farm in Australia and the family was about to go out to the cinema, but first we had to get my cousin's chickens inside. It was pretty difficult because you couldn't rely on a herding instinct to keep them together, so they trotted all over the place, scurrying in different directions. Eventually, we managed to get them rounded up and put away in their cages for the night. It had taken four of us to do it, but we made it to the cinema on time.

If you've ever been in a meeting, I'll bet you've been in a few where it felt like you were trying to herd chickens. Managing those people is for their own good too isn't it? Just as it was safer for the chickens to be in their cages where rats, snakes, goannas[1] and other beasties wouldn't be able to get to them, you'd expect people wouldn't want to waste their time in meetings. But how exactly do you herd chickens and still get to the cinema on time? That's what this book is about.

Let's see. Do you sympathise with any of these statements?

- I need to facilitate a workshop, but I don't know where to start or what I need to do.
- I've run a few workshops, but I don't know if I'm doing it right and assume there must be more to it.
- I need help managing troublesome behaviour.

---

[1] For those unfamiliar with Australian wildlife, a goanna is a carnivorous lizard with sharp teeth and claws that can grow up to 2.5m (eight feet) long. Aren't you glad you don't get them in your meetings?

- I can't seem to figure out how to get people to work through a problem.
- I don't even know what a workshop is, but I've heard they're cool.

If any of these are problems you're experiencing, then this is the book for you. My aim is to provide pragmatic advice which is of immediate use to both novice and practising facilitator. It can be read end to end, or you can dip into it depending on your need.

I tell you what I've found usually works and I warn you against things I think work less well.

The book is aimed at business users who have limited time and budget to achieve their objectives, but wish to do so in as inclusive, consultative, yet efficient a way as possible.

I've included advice and illustrative stories. In addition, there's a set of sample agendas to show examples of complete workshop processes. While they may not fit your own needs precisely, they will hopefully provide some inspiration and suggestions for how you could run some of yours.

Finally there's a short set of checklists and templates.

Facilitation and me

I first came across workshop facilitation in the early 1990s. Some colleagues partnered with a consultancy which used the approach to gather requirements and plan a project. My colleagues told me they reckoned I'd be able to do it when the next project came along. So I did.

Amazingly, it went very well, and so did the next one. After running about ten workshops, I was sent on a training course where I learned mainly about preparation. Because the course was videoed, I also learned that I waved my hand around as if I was stroking a cat on a chest high shelf. I stopped doing that pretty quickly.

After a few years, I began to train others. I ran hour long presentations, two day courses, three day courses and even a five day course. I continued to run workshops myself and to learn things. I still do.

I am facilitative by nature. I suspect I already was because I've usually been able to see more than one side of an argument. Added to that, work has probably rubbed off on my personality. It certainly comes out in my management style. I'm known for listening, suggesting alternative interpretations of behaviour (which I'm told is annoying when you simply want to be cross with someone), or pushing back on a hastily posed solution to be clear on what the problem actually is. I've even been known to facilitate conversations down the pub ("Hang on, just let him finish his point." "Oh shut up, Kev. We're not at work now.")

A process

This explains why workshops are important and how to go about making sure they happen.

There are no guarantees in this business. We're dealing with people and of course people can behave very differently depending on who they are, the situation in which they find themselves and what they feel like on that particular day.

The book is structured around the process of running a workshop.

Prepare

Chapter: Preparation

Define objectives and context	Agree with the workshop owner what the workshop is to achieve and why.
Identify participants	Who will attend the workshop and how do they feel about the objectives.
Decide date and time	Decide when the workshop will be held and how long it will be.
Invite participants	Invite participants to come to the workshop, providing them with any necessary background.

Chapter: Location and logistics

Find a location	Find a location for the workshop and an appropriate room.
Arrange local logistics and catering	Ensure the venue will be accessible, travel arrangements are in place, parking is available, catering is arranged.

Chapter: The workshop plan

Plan agenda Plan how the day will run and what materials will be required.

Plan room layout Plan the room lay out.

Run

Chapter: Starting the workshop

Set up Arrive in time to set up the room.

Introduce Once participants have arrived, set the scene, objectives and tone of the workshop and allow participants to get comfortable.

Chapters: Running the workshop and Challenging situations

Run workshop Run the workshop using the plan, managing both the process and the participants and achieve the required outcomes.

Chapter: After the workshop

Wrap up workshop Finish off the workshop, allocating actions and describing next steps.

Follow up

Chapter: After the workshop

Document workshop Document the workshop outputs as agreed with the owner.

Plan further workshops Ensure any lessons have been learned from this workshop and fed into further workshops, whether part of a series or not.

Break a leg

So read on. Workshop facilitation is both tiring and rewarding. I get a kick out of producing something in a given period of time, of solving problems and helping people to achieve their aims.

Workshop facilitation is an intellectual extreme sport in that, for all the planning, you're still dealing with uncertainty. But actually, isn't that just like life? And you've survived that so far.

Like other roles involving standing in front of a group of people such as teaching, lecturing, training or presenting, it's also a performance art so, as we embark on the experience of a workshop, I will leave you with the actor's blessing: "Break a leg!"

2

WHY USE A WORKSHOP?

What is a facilitated workshop anyway?

That's a very good question and in fact it means different things to different people. Here I will sigh and laboriously climb up onto my hobby horse and have a quick rant as to why everyone should see things from my point of view.

You see, the words "facilitator" and "workshop" are not protected words. Anyone can use them for anything. Both are used in other ways which can cause confusion.

When I first arrived in New Zealand and began to apply for roles as a business analyst, I had an interesting conversation with a recruitment agent.

"Why are you applying for business analyst roles when you're a trainer?" he asked.

This was a very puzzling question. I had been very careful to remove any mention of having run training courses from my CV precisely to avoid this potential confusion. What was he going on about?

"Well it says you're a facilitator," he explained.

I sighed. What was this man doing recruiting business analysts when he didn't know about one of the most important skills a business analyst should possess?

You see facilitator is often used to mean "teacher" or "trainer". A trainer or teacher often (or should often) use facilitation skills when teaching or training, but my gripe here is that there's a perfectly good word already for what they each do: "teacher" or "trainer".

But facilitate means to make easier. That's different to teaching and training. Which brings me onto "workshop".

Almost everything involving a group of people gets called a workshop. A training course for a start. A meeting, a presentation, a conference. Anything it seems where a group of people gather.

But a workshop is where something gets produced. A training course on the other hand, is where you are trained how to do something. A facilitated workshop is where *something is produced* and it's *made easier* for you by the facilitator. This is because the facilitator is ensuring there is a structure and a process to ensure a productive discussion.

If anyone wants to have a go at me about *my* use of the word "workshop", I am happy for them to do so if they work in a workshop with tools and stuff where they make actual things out of wood, metal or some other material. Most of what my workshop participants produce tends to be made out of brown paper and sticky notes.

Sadly, there's no standard agreed definition for facilitated workshop. It's probably easier to describe what one looks like.

You would see a group of people led by a facilitator who is neutral regarding the subject or problem being discussed. The group will be following a structure or process that has been designed and is now being led by the facilitator. There is likely to be information on the walls which represents what those people have discussed and agreed during the workshop.

Around that, there are many variables such as the number of people, the level of flexibility in the process, the way the people interact with the information on the walls and how much they run the process or move around the room. These will depend on the subject matter, the nature of the group, room and facilitator.

This book will help you think about those and other variables so that you can decide what they need to look like for any given situation.

Technology is easy...

Much, but by no means all, of my experience in workshop facilitation has been associated with technology projects. As you will have found yourself, technology problems are solvable. It's highly likely you will have experts in the technology available who can troubleshoot and come up with ingenious, and often simple, solutions to all the problems you come across. Technology either works or it doesn't.

I've often been at presentations, conferences or training courses, where the audience is asked for the kinds of problems that usually occur on projects. I'm sure you could make a list yourself, but here are some of the typical ones:

- Requirements were unclear or incomplete;
- The scope kept changing;
- People couldn't make up their minds;
- People weren't available when you needed them;
- Timescales were missed;
- People left the project or joined late;
- Communication was poor;
- The technology worked, but the business wasn't ready.

Notice a common thread? These are actually about people. It's very rare for someone to come up with an unsolvable problem around the technology. You might get one where new technology was introduced which no one understood or that was a wrong fit for the problem, but that isn't to say the technology was wrong, just that *people* made decisions that were perhaps not ideal.

So what we're getting down to is that people are the problem. People need to get better at working together. This isn't a new insight. It's been around for a long time, as any archaeologist digging up a skeleton with an arrowhead amongst the bones will tell you.

So here are some problem areas you'll typically find when working with people.

Focus: Any one person may be confused about what to work on or be distracted by something else which may or may not be work related.

Communication: There's always lots of information to impart, but are the right people being told, at the right time, in the right way, and how much is the message being lost in the blizzard of information people face every day?

Commitment: How interested is everyone in what you're doing and how important are the people who aren't that interested? Lack of interest can be driven by money, job security, career progression, profile of the project, distractions elsewhere...

Enthusiasm: Linked to commitment, however you can be committed, but not enthusiastic. ("I'm going to work late with you, but I really don't want to.") It can also wax and wane as the project progresses. Let's face it, some projects just go on too long.

Hierarchy: Some organisations are worse at this than others, especially if they're big on uniforms or job titles. This can affect freedom of thought and speech, who gets credit for ideas, who gets the blame when things go wrong, how quickly decisions are made and all those stories which you're thinking of right now.

Power: Linked to hierarchy, but not the same, because hierarchy is just one way of having power. Other ways are through knowledge or your job role; just think of those PAs or receptionists you can't get past. I always try to get to know support staff in an organisation. This is partly because they're in a position to make my life easier. It's also because they're usually nice people who I can have a laugh with about all the non-support staff who have their heads stuck up their backsides. Power can also be linked to how loud your voice is and even how much other people like you.

Consensus: Getting people to agree is rather tricky. People do insist on having their own points of view, often for quite ridiculous reasons. These include: it makes their job easier, it actually gives them a job, it makes sense to them, or they really don't understand what I'm talking about. Why these people can't just forget about their own failings and insecurities and agree with me, I really don't know.

Conflict: This doesn't usually involve physical violence, although bullying in the workplace is, sadly, far from rare. Usually it's simply about disagreement and it can manifest itself in heated debate, lack of listening, lack of commitment and enthusiasm, and of course pouting.

There are probably more, but you're depressed enough already, so let's move on.

What's wrong with meetings?

There are, as we'll see, some overheads in running a facilitated workshop and a related event has been in use for a much longer time and is very popular. Yes, it's the meeting.

Bored, feeling lonely? Hold a meeting. Many of us grow to resent them, but I've worked in organisations where people seem to love them. Invite ten people and another ten show up just to hear what's going on, or because they didn't think they'd find out what happened in any other way, or because they were passing the open door and it looked cool.

A new HR Director joined a large organisation and it didn't take him long to realise that there were an awful lot of meetings going on. Clearly a man with an enquiring mind and a dry sense of humour, he followed some people into a room and sat in during the whole meeting. No one questioned why he was there. At the end, everyone commented on what a good meeting it had been and went their separate ways. No one had been given any actions and he hadn't yet understood the point of the meeting

Informal research over the years has led me to the following list of things that go wrong in meetings, which I suspect will look familiar to you as well.

- Meeting goal is unclear;
- The agenda is vague or non-existent;
- Discussions ramble on for ages and one topic can take over the whole meeting;
- Participants aren't prepared for the discussion;
- Discussions go round and round;
- There are arguments but no debate;
- Certain individuals dominate, even if they don't mean to take over;
- No one checks on progress (assuming some sort of objective or agenda has even been established);
- There is no closure or actions.

Yes, we're getting depressed again. Of course what I'm talking about there are poorly run meetings. It's perfectly possible to have well-run meeting which do the opposite of the bullet points above.

Should I run a workshop or a meeting?

Meetings are effective when:

- You are providing information about events or the status quo, when it's largely one way communication, but more interactive than a straight presentation.
- You are gathering updates from individuals, but it's still a good idea to make sure they're relevant.

On one project I decided to have short, regular progress meetings. One of the main programmers (a reassuringly calm and weathered German who wore a comfortable woollen jersey and looked as though he ought to work in a submarine or a lighthouse) rolled his eyes at the idea of a meeting, but I insisted he came. I asked what everyone was working on, receiving quick updates. Then I asked if anyone had any problems. Two of them did, so I checked who needed to be present for that conversation and told everyone else they could go. The German looked surprised, then delighted and went and did some good work instead of staring into space. He did not complain about those progress meetings again.

On the other hand, if you are trying to solve a problem (defining it, coming up with suggestions, evaluating and discussing); trying to make a decision; managing many people; needing to be efficient; or there are politics to manage, you're better off running a workshop.

Workshops are successful (if run properly of course) because they have a number of magic ingredients:

- An owner of the workshop who also owns its objective and therefore has an interest in it being achieved;
- Agreed objectives and deliverables;
- A prepared process for achieving those objectives;
- That process is then followed; and
- There is an impartial, skilled facilitator.

Those all work for meetings too. The difference really is in the facilitator, because they are usually more active than the chair of the meeting. And usually more impartial too. I'll talk more about impartiality later.

Benefits of workshops

If your workshop is properly prepared and run, here are some of the benefits you can achieve from it:

- You will achieve your intended output and therefore have the result that justified the expense.
- The effect of working through issues together and coming up with a joint output is a great team building exercise to improve trust and cohesion.
- Your output will be of a higher quality because all of those who needed to be involved were involved, nutted out issues and ambiguities there and then, and agree with what was produced.
- This can have a marked effect on confidence, ownership and enthusiasm. Owning an outcome or a plan can have a marked effect on the way people go about doing their work which in turn can greatly influence the likelihood of success.
- Not only will your output be of higher quality, but it will probably have been created more quickly.
- If you want consensus, rather than compromise, it's probably going to be the best way to achieve it.

Uses for workshops

Given they are so effective, here are some uses for them:

Problem definition and resolution	Never underestimate the importance of ensuring you understand the problem and that everyone else has the same understanding of it. People not realising they are talking about different things is a common cause of disagreement.
Risk management	It takes many people to identify, assess and mitigate effectively.

Planning	If you want a plan that everyone buys into (and let's face it, it's the team who's delivering on the plan, not the project manager) then get everyone to plan the plan together. If you think that's obvious, then you haven't met the project managers who love their plan so much they write it like it's the next Great American Novel (or wherever you're from). Mind you, it will indeed be a work of fiction.
Test strategy	Defining a test strategy.
Processes modelling and analysis	Every stakeholder gets to see the end to end process and can give their own perspective and suggest improvements. Expertise for each part of the process is present and misunderstandings and issues can often be ironed out quickly.
Envisioning	Exploring and defining the vision for an organisation or a project.
Requirements gathering and prioritisation	Every stakeholder gets to understand the whole problem and see everyone else's point of view.
Retrospectives	Reviewing how something went. It could be an event, a deliverable or a project.
Prototyping	Plan their construction, design them, build them (depending on your technology) or review them.
Solution design	Workshops can be used at any level to design an entire solution architecture covering technology and non-technology or specific aspects of it. These often require several experts.
Options, ideas and creativity	Come up with and evaluate ideas, concepts or options.
Modelling data and functions	Create and model functions, use cases and data.

Assessments   Perform a health check, evaluate progress, assess a situation or identify whether your project is suitable for a particular project approach, such as an agile approach.

The facilitator

Like many jobs, there are some people who are better suited to workshop facilitation than others. You need to be able to structure your thinking and also be able to change direction and analyse situations quickly. You need to be calm, observant, a respectful listener, be able to see multiple points of view at the same time and have a good memory. You need to be a diplomat, a mediator, a referee, a guide, a pioneer even and a bit of a mug because it can be a very hard job with little thanks.

If it was a disaster, you might hear: "What a waste of time that facilitator was. I didn't know what I wanted before and I still don't!"

Even when a workshop is successful, sometimes it's just not obvious what you've done to contribute.

"It just goes to show - get everybody round the table, thrash it all out and come up with the requirements. But I still don't know why we needed that facilitator."

In general though, what you've done to ensure success should be clear. Then you're more likely to receive feedback like the following which was for one of the hardest workshops I've ever run. More on that one later too.

> *"Thanks VERY much for an excellent session yesterday. A lot of the people who attended have come up to me to say how good they thought the session was."*

Why use a workshop: Key points

- A facilitated workshop is where something is produced and it's made easier for you by the facilitator.

- Workshops are best used to help people work together more effectively.

- Workshops are effective because an independent facilitator creates a structure in which to discuss the content and actively monitors and manages that discussion as it progresses.

- Appropriately prepared and run, workshops can result in rapidly achieved, high quality outputs.

- Workshops have a wide range of uses.

3

PREPARATION

Never under-estimate the power of preparation. The best way to learn how effective it is, is not to do any. It should be obvious, but your workshop will run much more smoothly if you have a common goal, the right people, a process to work through, a comfortable room and all the supporting materials you need.

Effective preparation will help you think through what might happen and plan ways of dealing with it, preferably preventing those problems from occurring. Sometimes I will come out of a workshop thinking that facilitating a particular workshop was easy. Then I realise that this was because I clearly explained what was to happen and my planning had been thorough and effective. Of course workshops can still be hard to facilitate if you're as prepared as you could possibly be. It's just that they'd be much harder if you weren't.

I'm often asked how long should preparation take. Obviously there are many factors involved, including how well you know the subject area and participants, how complex the problem you're trying to solve, what materials you need to prepare, the nature of the participants and how much of the logistics you're required to do yourself. I know of a team of facilitators at a large bank who used to allow one day for each participant. I've sometimes taken a few days to prepare. This has included a number of meetings and sessions with colleagues to throw ideas around. I've also spent only a few minutes, but this has usually been for a subject matter with which I'm already familiar and people I already know.

As a rule of thumb, allow at least a day for your preparation and don't expect it to all happen during a single day. It will be spread across many.

Your preparation (or lack of it) will also be obvious to the participants. They will feel safe and trust a well thought out process and not feel the need to raise points in the wrong place, attack each other or some other worry which you're better off not having to deal with in the workshop.

Rudyard Kipling summarised the importance of questions in the following rhyme. It works well as a reminder for what you need to find out before a workshop.

> *I keep six honest serving-men*
>   *(They taught me all I knew);*
> *Their names are What and Why and When*
>   *And How and Where and Who.*

Let's start with the Why and the What: The context for the workshop and its objectives.

Objectives

What is the workshop for? What does it need to achieve? It's surprising how often your facilitation can start right back here on a one to one basis. Take this story for example.

> I had a manager once who would call me up.
>   "Kevin, I've got a great workshop for you to run."
>   "What's the objective?" I'd ask.
>   There would be a pause at the other end of the telephone.
>   "Ah yes...good question."

So, lesson one: You need an objective.

Ensure you understand what the objective is. If you don't understand it, there's no way you can get a room full of people to achieve it.

Like most objectives, it helps if it is SMART. There are a number of meanings for this acronym, but I'm using the explanations below.

Specific: Is it clear, rather than woolly; can you explain it back?

Measurable: The best test for whether something is specific is whether you will be able to tell when you've achieved it.

Achievable: Is it possible within the constraints, such as time?

Relevant: What is the context? Why is it needed? Now you know the context, does the objective still make sense?

Timebound: Should this be done now? What dependencies need to be achieved first? Does it have a deadline?

If your owner is struggling to define the objective, they may often have a better idea of what they want as an output. Work your objective backwards from that, even it's as simple as being able to create that deliverable.

Beware of when the owner has already decided what they want the outcome of the workshop to be and just wants to hold the workshop to pretend they're being consultative. Workshops generally create greater buy-in from participants, so if they come up with a different outcome to the owner's, what will the owner do? If it's to ignore any different outcome, advise against it. If that fails, suggest the owner presents his or her thinking and you can offer to facilitate the Q&A afterwards. If that fails, you may want to consider walking away as you might be tarred with the same brush as the owner.

The workshop owner was a director of the company. She sent me a two page briefing for the workshop. I read it several times and did not understand it. What was I to do? I didn't know her and I'd merely been nominated for the role. So what would she think of me, after she'd gone to the effort of writing me the brief, if I called her up and asked her to explain herself?

The answer was clear really. I could either risk designing the wrong workshop and look very silly on the day, or I could call her and deal with whatever happened. I called her. We had a conversation and I was able to check my understanding as we went along. The mud became clear water and the workshop went well.

If you're struggling to understand the brief, you really need to have an open discussion with the owner. As it is explained to you, it's much easier to ask questions as you go along than know where to start from a written workshop brief you don't understand.

Outputs

Make sure you have a clear understanding of what the outputs, the deliverables, are. If something similar has been done before, have a look at it. Check whether it needs to be exactly the same or whether they will accept improvements. If the output will form the basis of a document, look at the structure of the document and check whether you will need to populate each section during the workshop.

Participants

The owner

This is your main customer, the person who is sponsoring the workshop, possibly owning the budget which is paying for the workshop. They're the one who has a responsibility to see the problems resolved.

If there is more than one potential owner, make sure you know who your actual owner is. It is difficult to serve two masters. If there are contradicting demands, raise them and see that they are resolved.

The workshop owner can be used as a tie breaker, to underwrite decisions, to give guidance on objectives and scope and to back you up when dealing with awkward participants. Remember how useful they can be, but don't pay them so much attention during the workshop that you alienate other participants.

Subject matter experts

Identify who needs to come to the workshop. Often you will find that people are named as potential participants. You need to make sure they are the most appropriate ones. What is considered most appropriate will vary by workshop, but could include knowledge, enthusiasm, imagination, attitude or decision-making ability.

Try to identify the roles which need to be present, then put names on them. In some cases, someone may be able to play more than one role. Alternatively, if someone needs to drop out, it will be clearer who would make an effective replacement.

Consider whether different geographical locations need to be represented. Even if things really are the same everywhere, which is unlikely, some locations may resent other locations representing them e.g. the main office, the office in the capital or a rival city.

Ensure any relevant internal and external suppliers and customers are included. Cast the net wide for those who may be affected by the result to consider who should be invited. This may result in too many names, so later I suggest some ways to narrow the field.

> The National Resource Manager of a company was responsible for supplying team members for projects and managing the careers of those team members. He wanted to document the processes and requirements for his role to see what computer systems could be bought or developed to support him. The only other participants he wanted were the four regional Resource Managers.
>
> I asked whether his internal customers and suppliers should also be invited. As a result, the following people also came to the workshop: representatives of the projects who required staff who would actually be driving the requirements from their resource requests, the training manager and the union representative.
>
> All provided such valuable input that it was difficult to see what use the workshop would have been without them.

If anyone is being specifically excluded, find out why. If it is because they are thought to be difficult, but would otherwise be considered a valuable contributor, then ensure they are invited. It is your job as facilitator to control people who have been labelled as difficult. (See the chapter on **Challenging situations**.)

It is useful to find out what you can about participants, but realise you're only going to get opinions. I've often been warned about certain people who would be coming to a workshop ("Oh, look out, there'll be blood on the floor with him!") only to find that not only were they not difficult, but they were very well behaved and useful participants. If nothing else, including the troublemaker in the process means they are able to have their say and you ensure the discussion is fair. That way, supported or not, that person sees their idea has been dealt with properly. Left out, they run the chance of being a blocker to change after the workshop.

A potential explanation for this is that sometimes people are considered difficult because they keep going on about a particular problem. In the workshop they have no need to be difficult because at last their concerns are being heard.

Avoid too many participants. If someone is unhappy making decisions on their own, maybe they are the wrong person, but do not exclude the person with the knowledge if the decision maker does not have that knowledge themselves.

Representatives from a number of different helpdesks were brought together to agree the requirements for a common support tool. Every helpdesk but one had sent a manager and a customer service agent to the workshop to ensure decisions could be made and knowledge of how calls worked were both present.

The manager who did not bring one of her team said it would not be a problem because she knew what they all did. It soon became apparent that she did not know enough. This meant there was a risk that decisions would be made which would turn out to not fit with the needs of her helpdesk.

In this instance, it was fortunate that the workshop was being held in a room very close to where her helpdesk was situated. She was able to go out and fetch one of her team to field the detailed questions and the workshop continued successfully.

Bringing the right people is important because one of a workshop's strengths is that issues can get hammered out there and then rather than need to go through a lengthy review process afterwards with various people in different locations.

There is likely to be a mix of people of different seniority in a workshop. You will need to understand how this is impacted by the organisation's culture. I have known organisations where no one speaks until the senior person has spoken. This can be quite clear to observe because all heads will turn to look at the senior person in the room when a question is asked. You will need to deal with this and there is advice in the chapter on **Challenging Situations**.

Number of participants

How many participants should there be? How many do you need and how many can you handle? And what can you do if there are too many? When considering numbers of participants, you need to consider how they will respond to the size of the group. For a start, some of them will be intimidated by a large number and will speak less than they might have done otherwise, or at least, less frankly (see the chapter on **Challenging situations** for tips on how to handle this). Even if not intimidated, each participant simply may not have as much opportunity to participate as they would in a smaller group because there are more people with things to say.

In the picture below, there are only four participants. This is probably as small as you can go and still manage a workshop. You need to have enough to be able to stimulate ideas and discussion. Four people should be able to manage themselves, but it depends on personalities and the complexities of the problem. They may still need assistance working through a problem effectively.

This next one is usually a comfortable number, although of course it depends on your workshop and the participants. There are enough to get discussions going, but not so many that participants feel intimidated.

I used to say that twelve participants was the maximum number that anyone should facilitate effectively in one group. As it turns out, I've often facilitated more than this in a single group, but I would not like to have started out doing this. You can get a wide range of expertise and personality in a group this size.

Below is the largest workshop I have run without using breakout groups. In this instance I did it to maintain control over a very political group from many different organisations. It paid off, but I was exhausted by the end and had to be practically carried to the pub. My thighs were aching because I must have been tensing them all day, ready to manage the smallest dispute.

In the end, *you* need to be comfortable with the size of group. Here are some things you can do if you think the workshop will be too big a team.

- Reduce the workshop scope. This will hopefully also reduce the people required to discuss the new scope;
- Challenge the presence of each participant again;
- Try to double up people to cover more than one role;
- Run the workshop in breakout groups (see chapter on **Tools and Techniques**);
- Find someone else to run the workshop who is more experienced and able to deal with that many people;
- Turn down the workshop because you don't want to waste your customer's time and money and put your own reputation at risk if you don't think they will get the result.

Scribe

You'll be recording the progress of the workshop on wall charts of some sort (see later), but sometimes it can be useful to have someone else there taking further notes. Perhaps they will be responsible for producing the formal output.

Make sure they're briefed on how the workshop will run. During the workshop, you may want to check that they're writing down what you need. I sometimes make a point of asking the scribe to record something, usually if it is more detailed than I can record.

Sometimes it's just to get someone to shut up, as if I'm saying "See, it's on the wall and I've made sure the scribe's got it in detail too."

Some facilitators like to use the scribe to do all the writing which is visible to participants so that they are free to simply manage the discussion. I do not recommend this. If you use someone else to record the information on the wall, you are giving up some control. On the other hand, writing it down yourself, enables you to:

- pace how information is coming out so that you are not bombarded with it at too high a rate to record;
- ensure you heard it and everyone else did too (check if you think you missed something); and
- clarify anything which has been suggested which is or may be unclear.

Observers

An observer is someone who watches but does not contribute; they are there to watch and not say anything. This makes me wonder what the point of them is? If someone is there, surely they should participate. An exception could be a trainee facilitator, but you could still use them to scribe as it will keep them awake.

Occasionally, a senior manager will ask to come in and sit at the back out of interest, promising they won't say anything. How likely do you think that would be in practice? I suspect the other participants would feel rather uncomfortable having someone watching them behind their backs. If the senior manager is that interested, they should be invited as an active participant.

It's quite simple. If someone needs to be there, sit them amongst your other participants so they can join in discussion and you can manage them more easily.

In short, avoid having observers.

I've had observers a couple of times. Once they were trainee facilitators, who were well behaved but became drowsy. Here is what happened the other time.

Someone related to administering the project in question, but not involved in its content, wanted to come to the workshop out of curiosity to see the process. I was reluctant, but told him he could sit at the back of the room and he was to stay quiet. This didn't happen.

He interrupted 17 times. I know this because the scribe made a tally of how often he did it. I had a word with him in the morning break, but to no avail. He would simply begin each interruption with "I know I'm not supposed to say anything but..."

Now had he been adding something useful to the debate, I would have happily brought him into the workshop where he could contribute and I could manage him along with everyone else, but he wasn't. He was a very intellectual man and liked to wander off onto interesting, to him, side tracks. Initially I let these run to see where they were going to go, but soon realised there weren't useful. I could see that I had the other participants on my side because whenever the poor man opened his mouth, there would be a great deal of eye-rolling and slumping in chairs. He was sapping both time and energy in my workshop.

Fortunately, he was quite easy to deal with. He had a way of speaking whereby he would pause every few words as if seeking inspiration and allowing his words to fall like drops of gold for everyone. This meant it was simple for me to interrupt his slow sentence, finish it for him and move on before he knew what was happening.

It also helped that he was sat by an open window at the back of the room and traffic noise hindered his ability to hear. After lunch, happily full of food, he went to sleep.

Of course there I didn't dream of pointing this out to the other participants so I could use him to help a little team bonding with a shared joke...

The invitation

Once you know who all your participants are, you will need to invite them to the workshop. It is useful to have the owner send the invitation. Their name is likely to carry more weight than yours, especially if you are outside the organisation. Participants are more likely to make the time to come.

If possible, also have the owner, or of course their PA or other team member, coordinate participants' diaries and availability.

They have access to that information and it will save you a great deal of time.

The invitation may include a number of elements.

Date, time and place: Try to avoid Friday workshops because people are tired or may want to get away early. Be wary of running more than, say, three days of workshops in a week because it's very tiring for you, let alone your participants. If your workshop requires travel and an early start, consider going away the night before so that you are fresh and alert the next morning and have time to set up the room.

Objectives, scope and deliverables: Participants like to know what the workshop is all about and they will come mentally prepared. Being clear on the scope up front can help you manage scope creep within the workshop.

Context: If people have not been involved in this project or initiative before, it's useful for them to understand what it is all about by providing some background.

Participants: Everyone likes to know who else is coming. They may also provide feedback on whether you have the right people.

The agenda: The order in which things will be discussed. Make this brief and don't go into the detailed process description you made in your own planning. If a participant can only attend for part of the workshop, it is useful for them to know what they will miss and how much it will matter.

Pre-reading or preparation: If any work is required by the participants before the workshop, make this very clear. Also make it clear why it needs to be done. The amount you are able to do in the workshop may well hinge on this work being done, so be sure to do some contingency planning in case some or all participants do not do it.

How much should I know about the problem?

I am often asked this by trainee facilitators. The ideal facilitator is neutral. It is the facilitator's role to make discussion productive and to help that discussion along. The participants are the experts.

Therefore, you will need to understand the problem. As for content, I suggest you understand enough to avoid looking foolish, but not so much that you have an opinion which tempts you to join in the debate. Besides, I find that I may think I know the answer only to realise I don't when I start hearing people talking about an issue from their different perspectives.

While you are doing your preparation, take note of things people may say. Sometimes they will say something that would be useful to raise in the workshop. You can tell them that's it is just the thing you would like discussed in the workshop and ask them to make sure they remember to do so. You may also note it down. That way you can make sure it is raised and also show you were listening respectfully to them by saying something along the lines of "Sue, I know this was something you have concerns about..."

In some cases, they may not want to raise it themselves, so you may need to find a way to raise it yourself.

You can also note down any examples you come across. Some of these may be useful to start off a brainstorm when people are still nervous of being the first to speak and wondering if they know the kind of thing you're asking them to suggest.

Preparation: Key points

- An effective owner will own the problem, set the objective and be open to suggestions.

- Participants need to be knowledgeable in their subject area and be able to make any expected decisions without recourse to parties outside the workshop.

- You need to be comfortable with the number of participants who are coming.

4

LOCATION AND LOGISTICS

On site or offsite

The first decision, which may well have been made for you, is whether to hold the workshop on the customer's premises or offsite, for example at a hotel, a conference centre or community facility.

Below are some things to consider when choosing between them:

On site

- Usually free;
- Easy for participants to find and access;
- Easy for participants to be distracted by their usual jobs;
- Normal surroundings may not inspire creativity.

Off site

- Costs money;
- Usually comes with a dedicated support team;
- Is neutral ground if required;
- May require extra effort to get to and find, so extra information needs to be given to participants;
- Can be seen as showing how much the company values the workshop's output because it is prepared to pay extra to achieve it;

- Can be more interesting for participants because it is a day out of the office.

As I describe below, if no suitable rooms are available, you may wish to revisit the location.

Room shape

The room you use is very important. A poor room can make life difficult for you. In my experience, it can make it harder than the people. Sadly, most meeting rooms are designed for just that: meetings. People are expected to sit around a table in the most unimaginative way.

Here's a common meeting room layout:

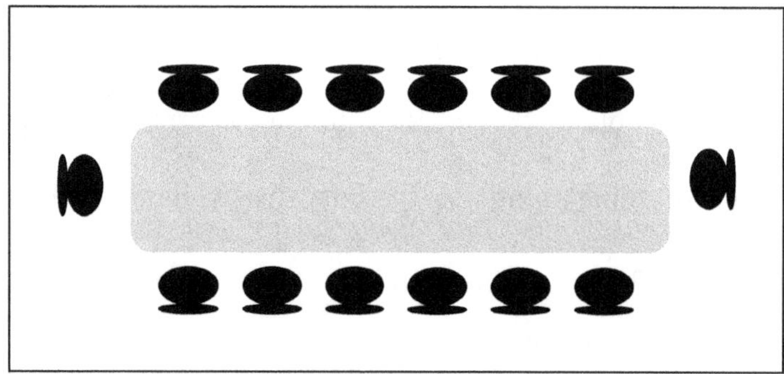

While it's great for a big meal, it's not ideal for a workshop. You could facilitate a meeting and record things right behind you or in a document which has been projected onto a wall.

I've often been given workshop rooms like his though and I've managed like this.

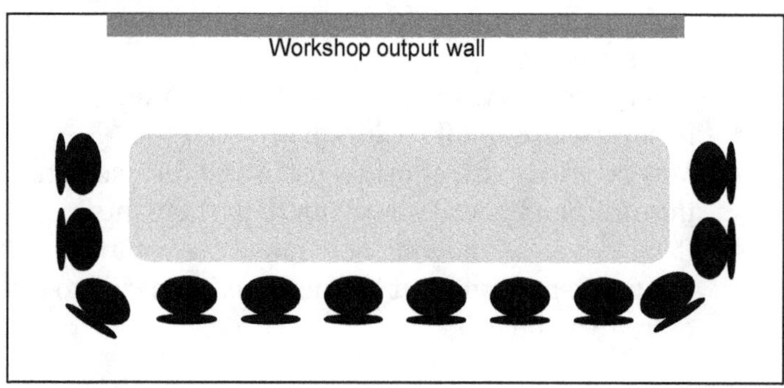

It's a bit cramped and it's hard for everyone to have a good view of everything which is on the display wall, but you do what you can. The worst examples of this have been either very narrow or very long, both of which made it really hard for everyone to see and the former made it hard for me to even move around much.

Here's another of my favourite terrible rooms:

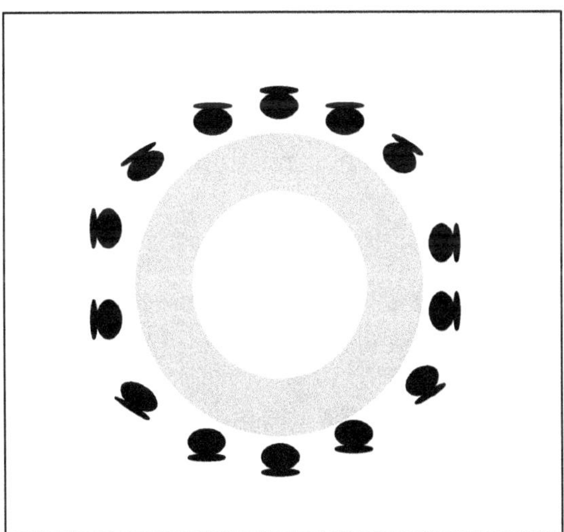

And here's how we ended up:

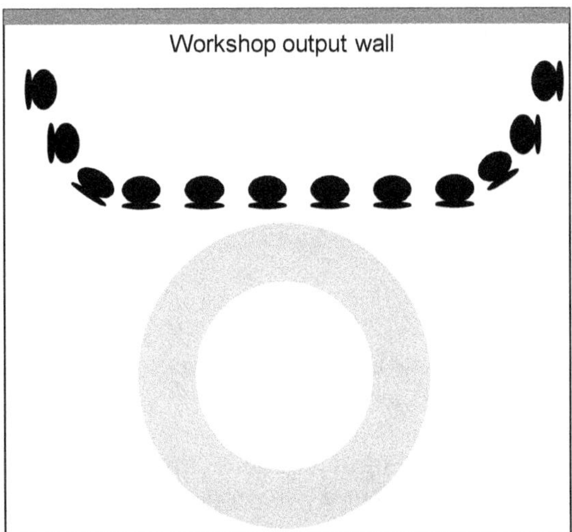

With a circular table in the workshop room at the customer's offices, I was faced with a problem. I could stand in the middle and at least be able to be close to people, but I would not be able to record anything on the wall. Alternatively, I could seat people around one side of the table, but they would be both a long way from me and from the workshop output wall.

The solution was to move the table out of the way. This proved to be rather tricky because the table was heavy. I heaved against it. It moved a little way. Something seemed to be stopping it. I looked underneath to see if I could see what it was.

To my horror, the top of the table legs had moved, but not the bottom. The legs were now at a very unhealthy angle and some of the screws holding them on were popping out of the underside of the table. Swearing quietly to myself, I straightened up all the legs.

I had just finished when the door opened and in walked the facilities manager who had shown me to the room.

"What are you doing?" he asked.

"Moving the table out the way," I replied.

"You can't do that, it's a boardroom table," he replied.

I paused for a moment, trying to understand why a boardroom table could not be moved, but others, presumably could. I still haven't worked it out.

"We should put it back," he continued.

"No," I said, perhaps a little too hastily. "We might as well leave it where it is now. I've barely moved it yet."

To my relief, he agreed and left. I decided not to try to move the table any further back in case all the legs came off. Instead, I moved the chairs into a narrow ellipse facing the wall.

My ideal layout is something like the picture on the next page. Benefits offered by this layout include:

- Everyone faces the wall and can what's displayed on it;
- Everyone can see each other;
- No one is at the head of the table;

- The facilitator has space in which to move around and is able to approach people individually if required;
- If there is room behind the U-shape, it can be used for group work.

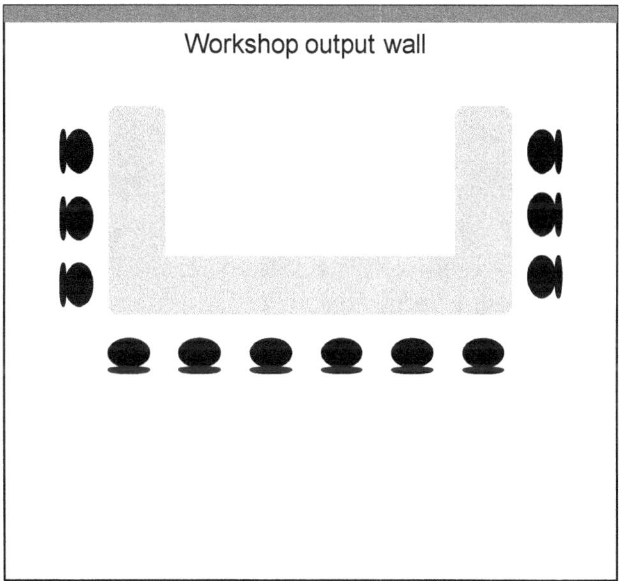

Another layout for group work is to have separate tables as in the picture below.

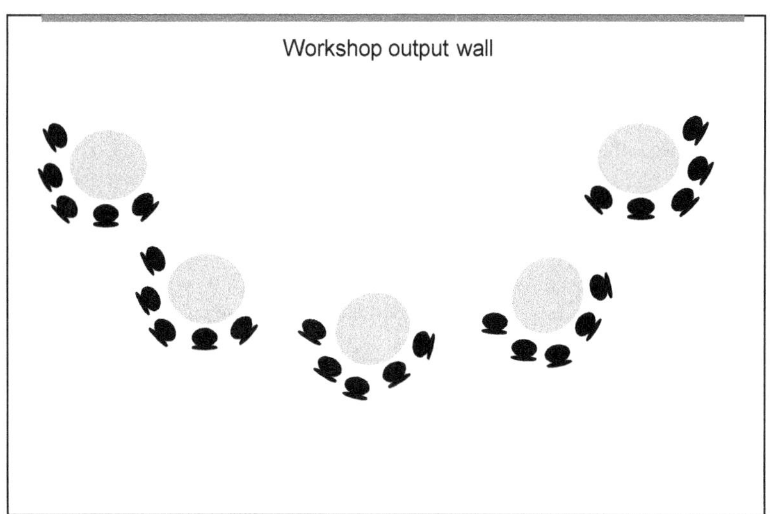

The U-shape enables everyone to see each other and the display wall. It also allows the facilitator to move around the room and get close to people, which can be a benefit when encouraging participants to say less or more (see chapter on **Challenging situations**).

I was staying at the hotel where I was to run a workshop the next day and asked the facilities manager to show me the room they had designated. It had a meeting room table the size of Wales, with chairs dotted around its extremities like offshore islands. I would have been unable to get close to people which would have decreased my ability to manage them in the event I needed to.

I asked if there were any other rooms available. She looked a little disappointed and showed me one the same size, but made up of tables which could be moved around. I was delighted and used that one instead.

The blank wall is to be covered with a working backdrop of brown paper or flipchart sheets. If there are no blank walls, it's possible to use mobile notice boards.

I have found that there are many interpretations of what constitutes a blank wall. Some I have come across have, for example, turned out to be scattered with paintings screwed to the wall, have a door in it or a bookcase.

The blank wall, even when blank, can be made up of a whole range of materials, some of which can be a challenge to the adhesive effects of masking tape or wall tack.

While painted plaster is the most common, I have also come across cloth covered movable partitions, wood, glass, brick and even strange, textured, furry wallpaper.

For the wall paper room, I hung one sheet of brown paper from a painting and another on the back of a door. Fortunately, this was all I needed. I got around the brick wall and a lack of masonry nails and a hammer in my workshop kit by hanging the brown paper from the metal ceiling tiles.

Clear, sticky tape works well on glass, although can leave marks. If in doubt, check with someone responsible for the facilities about what you can use, although I have heard it suggested that it is better to ask for forgiveness than permission. I will leave that to your judgment in the circumstances in which you find yourself.

One hotel in which I was running a workshop objected to me using either masking tape or wall tack as they said it would pull paint off the walls. I was surprised because this had never happened in all my years of using it. They offered me an alternative from their own supplies which was a strong sticky pad which needed to be pressed onto the wall, but could also be removed afterwards. I used it and it held the brown paper onto the wall successfully.

The first sticky pad I removed from the wall at the end of the workshop, took off not only the paint, but a lump of plaster underneath. I was glad I had used their suggestion.

Size of room is another one to watch out for. Many organisations include the number of people a meeting room can hold in their room descriptions. Bear in mind this is usually the number that can fit in a room when sat around a table as if they are going to eat dinner. You are likely to need a much bigger room.

You'll need to visit or see a picture of the room as early as possible to allow the room booking to be changed if required.

Visiting it yourself is obviously the better option as it will better enable you to check its size will work for the number of people and style of workshop, whether the furniture is suitable, position of power sockets, if required, whether technology such as screens and projectors actually work, and whether you'll be able to get into it at the time you need it.

Other technicalities which can cause frustration are not having the right connectors or not knowing how to use any of the kit. It's often much easier if you can do without technology.

Check that the room has power points where you need them, that the chairs are comfortable enough to sit in for the duration of the workshop and that the room has natural light as this is more likely to keep people awake than artificial light.

Try to book the room for at least an hour before you intend to use it, or more if you have an elaborate set up. Make sure you are able to access the room as well. It's very annoying when you get up early to prepare for your workshop only to find no one is on Reception yet when you arrive.

Be prepared to re-arrange the room's furnishings. A meeting room in a provincial English hotel was full of ornate gold painted furniture which I'm sure was quite classy, but as far as I was concerned it was in my way. I shoved most of it against the walls, which rather surprised one of the hotel staff when he came in to refresh jugs of water at a break.

Even if you have provided detailed guidance on how you would like the room set up, such as a diagram, this may not be well communicated to those who are actually setting up the room.

I had requested a projection screen. I had assumed I would be given one on a stand like your Dad used when showing you his slides when you were a kid (depending on how old you are) or which could be unrolled from a special holder on the wall.

We arrived to find a huge construction bolted together out of metal into what amounted to a temporary cinema screen. It was only required for a short presentation at the start of the workshop, after which we were to make use of the blank wall behind it, but the cinema screen obscured the wall. Fortunately I had arrived early and was able to ask for the monstrosity to be removed. Two roadies duly appeared and began to unbolt the screen, then a small folding screen was brought which did the job perfectly well.

It is best therefore to not only explain what you want, but why you want it and how you're going to use it. Do remember that facilities managers are usually trying to be helpful and will offer you their best rooms where they can. Like any support staff, these people can be your greatest allies. They can make the difference between heaven and hell as far as your workshop goes. Make friends, bring them into your confidence, be polite. If you use a venue often, they will come to understand your whimsical needs. They will appear magically with extra flip charts and pens, they will smooth the arrival of refreshments. In short, they will enable you to focus on the workshop instead of the logistics.

A workshop had about 30 participants from many different organisations. It was intended to deal with a major problem with national visibility where two groupings of companies were at loggerheads. It was going to require creativity in an environment rife with politics and egos.

I was offered a large meeting room which would have done for half the number of participants, but this number was going to be squashed and uncomfortable.

I explained the effect of the room and suggested that if they were serious about solving the problem, then they needed to give people room to think.

The sponsor agreed to pay a substantial amount to hire a large room. Although very spacious, it was underground and therefore lacking in natural light. This meant that mobile phone reception was weak, but we saw that as a benefit as it would help to keep participants focused.

In the situation above, I was lucky that the customer agreed to find a new room, but usually you will have no choice but to work with the room you are given. If you really think the workshop will actually fail if it is run in a certain room, then say so, otherwise you can only warn of reduced quantity or quality of output. Whenever I complain about a room, I feel that I am acting like some prima donna. Your objections certainly need to be clear to overcome any raised eyebrows. That being said, you need to do the best you can to overcome the failings of a room and that means knowing those failings as early as you can.

Logistics

Beyond the room, there are other things you need to worry about.

Ensure that parking is arranged if required. Make sure the building's reception is warned that participants are coming. If there are large numbers, see whether Reception will prepare visitors badges to speed up registration or sign in. They will often prefer it and it will avoid participants being delayed at reception.

Decide if you need refreshments and work out how to source them and who is paying. Make it clear what refreshments are being provided. If people think they're getting lunch and they're not, you may lose affection, people, or at least time, when they have to go and get something to eat. It's also amazing what people will do for food. I'm amused at how often it is used in lieu of pay for extra time at work. Early meetings are rewarded with muffins and late ones with pizza. Incidentally, I don't recommend this as a long term diet.

If there is a need for photocopying, printing, extra stationery, make sure you know the process for obtaining it.

Responsibility

One last thing to say around logistics. You can delegate as much as you can to others to prepare your materials, arrange the room, design bits of prepared paper to hang on the walls and make sure all your materials arrive at the venue. But think about who is going to have to cope if things go wrong. Yes, it's you. So it's down to you to make sure that the way things have been done meets your needs. It's your responsibility, because you're the one who's going to have to deal with it.

Preparation: Key points

- A workshop typically requires twice the space normally allocated to a meeting room for the same number of participants.

- Arrive in time to set up.

- Parking, access to the building or room and catering can limit the effectiveness of your workshop if not arranged properly.

5

THE WORKSHOP PLAN

At the heart of your preparation is your workshop plan. This needs to be more detailed than simply saying we're going to talk about A, B, C and D, which is all you would see in most agendas. You need to cover how you're going to talk about them and how you will record it. This can range from simple to complicated.

In Appendix I, I've included a set of example agendas. These are based on real agendas which have worked. Just bear in mind that no two workshops are the same and chances are that, if you use them, you'll need to adapt them for your particular circumstances.

I've seen what I'm about to talk about given a number of different names: scripted agenda, workshop process, run sheet, workshop plan. You can call it what you like. Just do one.

There are a number of places the workshop plan can come from. It can come from a previous workshop you've run, a colleague, a book or simply from your own imagination. I've spent five minutes coming up with one and I've also spent five days including multiple meetings. It depends entirely on the workshop and situation.

Consider your inputs:

- Objectives;
- Deliverables;
- Length of workshop;
- Room size and layout (Is there room for breakouts? Will everyone be able to see outputs on the wall?;
- Number of participants (Will it need one group or teams?);

- Nature of the participants (From what you know, are they likely to be helpful or argumentative; obsessed by hierarchy and rank; how well they know each other?)

Plan for interim deliverables

Think about the process in logical steps. Left to themselves to run their discussion, people will think in different ways, at different speeds and quite probably miss out important factors. You're trying to get them to think about one thing at a time, because that's easier, and then gradually pull the threads together.

Ensure that you provide useful outputs along the way. Many of them will be used as an input to the next stage of the workshop. This way, if you run out of time, you have still delivered something useful which can be taken forward later. Also, having participants consider only a small part of the problem at a time, makes it easier for them (and that's what facilitate means). Here's an example.

You're running a risk management session. The outputs are a set of risks for a project with mitigating or preventative actions, as well as a prioritisation which is usually based around the likelihood of something happening together with the impact if it does.

Here are two approaches:

Approach 1

Step	Interim deliverable
Identify first risk Decide its likelihood Decide its impact if it happened Define action plan to prevent or mitigate the risk.	First risk managed
Identify second risk Decide its likelihood Decide its impact if it happened Define action plan to prevent or mitigate the risk.	Second risk managed
Etc	

I don't recommend that approach. How long do you spend on any one risk? Say you have a two hour workshop and the first risk takes half an hour to discuss. How do you know that you've got all the risks out when two hours are up?

Below is the approach that I recommend using instead. This focuses on finishing one task at a time.

Approach 2

Step	Interim deliverable
Do an initial brainstorm of all risks.	Risk list
Prioritise each risk by likelihood and impact.	Prioritised risk list
Identify which risks are the most important to be managed.	Shortened list to manage
Define action plans to prevent or mitigate each risk. Do this priority order.	Completed risk management plan

Using this approach, gives you the following benefits.

You know how many risks you have to deal with	Knowing this means that you can pace yourself or manage expectations about whether you're going to be able to get through everything in the time allotted. And if it took you the whole workshop to get to this point, you've still got a useful output of all your risks identified. These can be usefully taken forward. If you had taken the first approach, you would end up with only part of a list of still undetermined length.
You can work in priority order	Knowing your high priority items, you can work on those first. If you hadn't already agreed it with your workshop owner, you may even decide with them now that you won't bother discussing

> how to manage the lower priority ones.
> Again, you have a useful interim
> deliverable which can be taken forward.

Not only are you as a facilitator getting the benefits above which help you run the workshop effectively, but you're also helping the participants by getting them into a pattern of thinking for each stage of the agenda. They only have one problem to solve at a time.

Plan how you will use the space and the room

Once you've figured out how you're going to break down your process, think about how that's actually going to look in your workshop; how you're physically going to manage that process. What are you going to use? How will the information you're gathering build as the workshop progresses? How will you take the outputs from stage 1 and use them in stage 2?

To take the example above, if I write down all my risks on a flip chart, how will everyone keep them in mind once I've turned the page, how will we prioritise them and where do I write the managing actions? If I have used our great friend the sticky note, I can re-order them, combine them, place them on a chart or associate them with a whole bunch of managing actions.

This assumes that you're going to use the wall to capture your outputs, but they can also be spread out on a table or on the floor.

Will you need to prepare any charts or provide supporting materials? Can these be made on the day or do you need to create them in advance? Make sure you know how these are going to reach your destination. If they are not travelling with you, allow plenty of time for couriers. You may also consider what you are going to do if they do not arrive on time or even at all.

I had travelled to a workshop by train and so had couriered both my workshop kit, which was in a large toolbox, and a large roll of brown paper. The paper arrived, but by the morning, the toolbox had not. This contained all my note paper, masking tape, spray glue to make the note paper stick to the brown paper, and pens.

I asked someone in the office if there was an office supply shop nearby and there was. The workshop started at 9.30am.

> I hoped the shop opened at 8.30. I had just enough time to nip out and buy the materials I needed.

These days I carry only what I need so that it's always with me and it's years since I've needed to courier anything. You can still be caught out.

> A colleague and I were flying domestically for a workshop that day. We had some prepared brown papers rolled up in a plastic tube. At the check-in desk, we were told that the tube was too long to take as cabin baggage. Our tickets were without baggage so we had to pay extra to have it carried under the plane in both directions.

When working through how your information will flow or how you will make use of the wall space available, I often find it useful to sketch out what it will look like and where different sections of information will go. I'll do this on a piece of paper, a whiteboard or even in presentation software.

You want your information to build as the workshop progresses. Sometimes I'll take some stickies from one stage and reuse them in the next, perhaps plotting them on a chart.

When working with groups, each has their work area, usually in a corner. When each group presents on the work they've been doing, the larger group wanders from corner to corner to hear them.

Different parts of the room can become associated with different stages of the agenda and different thought processes: no criticism in this part of the room thank you, just ideas.

In the example below, I worked out what colour stickies I was going to use for different pieces of information, that some information would be framed on a flipchart sheet, where a diagram was going to be created as we went along and even where a fixed cabinet was that I wanted to avoid when I was putting things on the wall for most of the day.

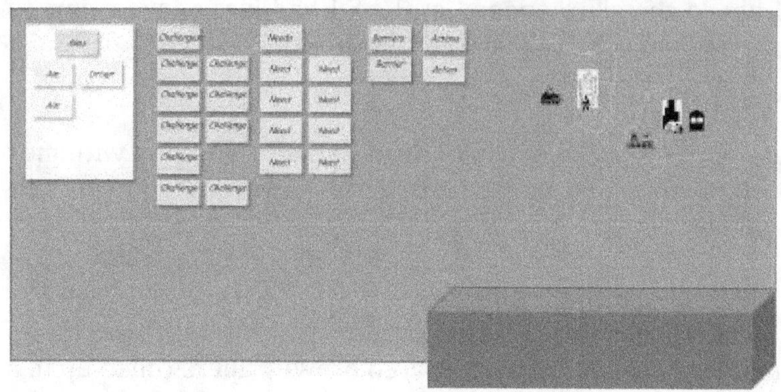

Team considerations

The facilitator helps participants work together as a team for the duration of the workshop. You may not be able to create a fully functioning team in the time available to you, but you need to do enough to achieve your objectives. You may be working with anything from an existing team to a room of complete strangers. How you structure your agenda may well be affected by this.

Consider a workshop where some or all participants are unknown to each other. They don't know what the other participants are like, how they think, what they know or how much they can trust them. On top of that, they may be nervous about the purpose of the workshop, how well they can contribute to it or how much they will understand or what they are expected or able to provide as input to it.

This seems like quite a tough mountain to climb, but there are things you can do.

Pre-workshop briefing	Provide a briefing before the workshop explaining its purpose and content.
Warm up exercise	Warm up exercises or icebreakers can break down barriers, get people focused and provide some social levelling.
Explain the approach as you go	Ensure explanations for what is expected at each stage of the workshop are clear. Monitor how they progress so you're able to step in and provide guidance or change the approach.

Introductions	Introduce the participants to each other.
Explain objectives	At the start of the workshop, explain the objectives and approach.
Make discussions respectful	Manage discussions to ensure interactions are respectful and that all opinions are heard.

From this you could conclude that the facilitator may be quite active at the start of the workshop.

As the workshop progresses, participants become more comfortable with each other and with the process so will often need less facilitation. Between these two there may well have been any number of interventions, for example, to explain an exercise, to refocus a conversation, defuse an argument or prevent someone from being shouted down.

What is discussed can even have an effect on this. The workshop will begin with some ritual: explaining objectives, introductions. This is low risk and begins to allow people to settle in. The rest of the workshop deals in facts, opinions, feelings and decisions.

Facts are relatively low risk. They are things which are known. In expressing opinions, people are beginning to expose themselves. A fact can be referenced, but an opinion cannot and may be challenged or lead to someone making a judgement about the person who expressed the opinion.

To allow yourself to express feelings can lead to further judgement. You are showing part of your personality that is more intimate. Finally, decisions can be referred back to, they may turn out to be ill-judged, or believed to be. They can be perceived to be dangerous.

If they do not know each other, participants are unlikely to want to make decisions early on in the workshop when they neither know people nor are confident about the process. Later in the workshop, they will hopefully have become more comfortable. So, have the lower risk, fact based discussions at the start of the workshop when people are still getting to know each other. Save the higher risk opinions and decisions for later when people are more comfortable.

Fortunately, many workshop processes will naturally follow this path. Following the ritual opening, there may be a gathering of facts. Some form of brain storm or idea generation can be judged as low risk because it is a deliberate creation of many ideas. This provides an atmosphere in which people can begin to get to know one another and understand each other's background.

This can then be followed by some sort of analysis or investigation where opinions and reasoning begin to be expressed. Again, gradual trust is being built as people's motivations begin to become clear.

Finally there may be some decisions made. Here is where people are expressing their feelings, but by this stage in the workshop, they should be more comfortable with each other and be prepared to come out with more strongly held thoughts. Ensure you allow enough time for discussion.

It follows then that you should consider the comfort of your participants when designing your process. Check whether they are going to be ready at a particular point in the agenda to handle the task you are setting.

A government was trying to bring in the use of PINs at point of sale. Retailers and banks had been told by the government that if they did not implement it on their own, they would be forced to do it through legislation. The company I worked for was working with banks and retailers, but both parties were at loggerheads and had been so for perhaps months.

The banks were saying they would not put out cards which could be used to take a PIN rather than a signature until there were enough terminals out there to make it worthwhile.

On the other hand, the retailers were saying they wouldn't install terminals until there were enough cards out there that could use them.

I was asked to run the workshop to try to resolve this issue. After much thought, the approach I used turned out to be remarkably simple. I had each side explain why they were taking this stance.

This gave the other party an understanding of the other side's problems. While this did not make those problems ago away, it did mean that each side stopped seeing the other as being awkward. Instead, they saw them as reasonable people dealing with issues just like they were.

Those problems became common targets to resolve and resolve them they did. I overheard one participant saying to another during the morning break that he had not realised the other party was under a particular constraint before.

It was one of the most exhausting, rewarding and exhilarating workshops I have ever run.

Involvement

Think about ways of getting participants out of their seats during the workshop or of getting them more involved. For example making them sort sticky notes on a board as a group will provide physical stimulation after sitting down, give them extra involvement in the creation of a deliverable and a different, physical way of thinking about it. I prefer to have people out of their seats and physically active if possible because they become more mentally active as well. They are actually working together, moving things, discussing, pointing and working as a team.

Presenting information in a pictorial or graphical way can be more interesting and have more impact than simply listing on flipcharts. Colour is also stimulating.

Missing participants

Beware of when a participant cannot be in the whole workshop, but is vital for at least part of it. This becomes a planning constraint. If it doesn't work, consider re-scheduling the workshop. This is far better done weeks before the workshop happens rather than on the day.

Typical activities

There are different kinds of activity that can happen in a workshop. Sometimes the workshop may be about only one of them. In others it could encompass them all. The following list looks at a set of activities which are common to many workshops. Think about which ones are likely to happen in your workshop and how you propose to deal with them.

Find a structure that works	Ensuring you have coverage of potential information is usually vital, so find a model to help drive it out. This could be a high level process model, a breakdown of a problem, or a model such as SWOT or PEST which looks at a topic from multiple perspectives (see **Tools and techniques** chapter). You may define this structure during your preparation or the workshop. If the former, you can still validate it during the workshop.
Decide how to gather information	Decide out how to extract information from participants. The old favourite is the facilitator at the front leading the participants and putting up the output on the wall, but there are other ways. A first cut could be presented from research or participants could be tasked with creating it themselves and having it reviewed and challenged afterwards. If this latter is used, it may be worth starting out with the facilitator leading to demonstrate the level of detail required and how they need to think.
Stage and pace the process	When dealing with difficult subjects, such as a negotiation, be careful not to move too quickly. Take participants step by step to keep them with you.
Define categories	If information is to be shaped, framed or grouped in some way, these categories could be defined as part of preparation or allowed to evolve in the workshop.
	Be clear over whether the partitions in your model are fundamental or there simply to help frame thinking and drive out information. If the latter, it doesn't ultimately matter in which part of the model particular information appears, only that it is there.

Gain opinions	Allow time for people's opinions to be aired and recorded. There may be a way of displaying these opinions which shows the limits of any disagreement. It'll also show where there is agreement. If people can see they aren't completely at odds, it can help them become reasonable in other areas.
	Give people the opportunity to try out ideas. Give them a chance to think about them and to test them through scenarios or examples.
Define the problem	A common cause of conflict is not being clear on what your disagreement is. Indeed, if a problem is perceived differently by each party, it's going to be an uphill battle resolving the problem to the satisfaction of all parties.
Allow for discussion	People need time to talk, so make sure there's time allowed for it in the agenda.
	Sometimes people just need to talk. You may have already covered off what they're going to say, but giving them time to say it as well can be time well spent because they either need to vent their feelings or talking about an idea is their way of buying into it by claiming it as their own in adding their thinking.
Let people vent	If people need to get something off their chest, let them. They'll feel better for it. I've even allowed a specific section of the workshop to bitch and moan. Sometimes you don't even need to do anything with it, although it's effective to refer back to the complaints to acknowledge them or to show how they're being dealt with.
Identify options	There may be options for a decision. Identify as many as are reasonable and

explore each one. Combining options is often possible, or at least parts of them. Encourage participants to be as creative as they can in coming up with options for solutions, challenge assumptions. Even a seemingly extreme solution may have something in it which can be used.

Methodically remove disagreements

People form opinions and can take some shifting from them. Wars have been fought and millions have died because sets of people have different opinions. As a facilitator, you can make your contribution to world peace by trying to deal with conflicting points of view. When people have objections, ensure you deal with each of those objections one by one, understanding them and identifying whether you can eliminate any of them.

Ensure responses are balanced

People can praise without seeing the downside or they can be completely negative, seeing only what's wrong. Set aside time to work through all points of view and prepare some challenges in case participants struggle with the opposing viewpoint.

Avoid group think and make dissent safe

One person can set a tone. Their view may be so convincing that other participants don't even try to think of counter-arguments, or may not risk voicing their opinions. Peer pressure is a wonderful thing. If everyone else in the room appears to be completely agreed on a point, only the brave or very confident are likely to disagree.

This makes it your job to suggest alternatives, challenge, probe, come up with scenarios, measures and what ifs to ensure opinions are tested. You need to support dissent or notice anyone looking uncomfortable and encourage them to speak up.

When agendas fail

While my title sounds like one of those late night television programmes, agendas *will* fail to a greater or lesser extent. I have rarely, if ever, stuck precisely to a plan. As Helmuth von Moltke the military strategist said: "No plan survives contact with the enemy." Not that you should think of workshop participants as your enemy of course.

Often it's the approach that you need to change rather than the objective. You must be prepared to adapt to changing circumstances rather than insisting on forcing your agenda through. These can arise for a number of reasons:

- A business issue comes up that you weren't expecting and you need to deal with it;
- You haven't done enough preparation and there's something you haven't thought of;
- Participants you weren't expecting show up;
- Some participants don't show up.

You can't avoid all problems, but you can limit the number which will occur. In the worst case scenario, you may need to stop running the workshop because it has become irrelevant or you need to start all over again with different people and a new process.

There have been times when I've over-planned a workshop when the participants were actually able to move at a faster pace. In one example, all we needed was someone to put up a draft solution. That started the debate and provided the foundation for what was agreed by the group.

The following example happened for a different reason as you will see.

I was running a series of post implementation reviews of a troubled project which had just done the first of a number of rollouts across the country. We had run seven out of eight with different teams and all had followed the same plan:

What went well (a surprise that anything had)

What did not go so well;

What could we do to keep doing things that went well;

What can we do to avoid the bad stuff during the next phase.

This one was different. Previously, participants had been able to express the first two steps in the process in pithy bullet points (which I could easily translate onto a sticky note). These ones rambled on at great length about issues.

I realised that these guys weren't bothered about how the project had gone. Now it had finished, they had found they were simply unable to do their job properly. As far as they were concerned, everything was broken and the project wasn't finished.

I had morning coffee slightly earlier than planned and conferred with my colleague and the workshop owner. We decided we would not follow the usual agenda. Instead we would use the workshop to document their concerns. They turned out to be vital.

In a follow up meeting we agreed that the implementation had been so poor, the business in that part of the country was going to go bankrupt in about two weeks. Had I not been prepared to adapt my approach, we might not have found this out in time.

We quickly planned a further workshop to look at rolling back the new solution to the old system again while it was fixed. I'll tell you more about that in *Breakout groups* in **Tools and techniques**.

The main thing to realise is that your agenda is merely a tool to accomplish the objectives. If it turns out to be the wrong tool for whatever reason, make yourself a new one. The objectives are what is important, not your agenda. If you need to, give yourself some time to think of how you're going to run your approach. Use the participants to help you, if required.

Document the plan

I use a template for my workshop plan. Sometimes I don't need to go as detailed as my template allows, but it helps me make sure my approach works. I use a table because I like things in tables. What yours looks like doesn't matter, but if you're a new facilitator, I recommend you do write it out. It will help you get your thinking straight because writing out to this level of detail forces you to analyse your process.

Stage of the process	The agenda item, briefly explaining what this part of the workshop is about.
Approach	Break down that stage of the workshop into the steps you're going to follow. Include how you will deal with this physically and any tools or techniques you'll use, including whether this will be full group or breakout group. Include any comfort or meal breaks.
Deliverable	The output of each workshop stage.
Completion time	By writing down the time when I think this part of the workshop will finish, I give myself a quick reference guide to how well I'm tracking during the workshop and it keeps me aware of my deadline. If I meet my interim deadlines, chances are I'll meet my final one of the end of the workshop.
Time taken	Define how much time you're going to allow for each step.

This plan is mainly for your use and for any co-facilitators or note takers. You should also go through it with your workshop owner so they know what they're getting and can confirm you're on the right track to solving their problem. It builds confidence for both of you.

Avoid sharing anything too specific about timing with participants. You may apparently be behind schedule, but know how you can catch up by trimming times or leaving out steps which you know are of lesser importance. They, on the other hand, may stop focusing on the workshop and start worrying about how long there is still to go or whether they'll catch their bus or be able to pick up the kids from school in time.

What you could still share is what you're going to handle before a break and what after it. You may also state how long you're going to take over a particular stage of the workshop. This can be useful if you're going to deliberately timebox discussion i.e. "We're going to see where we get with this in half an hour, but will call a halt to it after then even if we haven't got to the bottom of it."

As a minimum, share a brief description or title of each stage with participants. Then you will need to explain each stage of the process as you get to it so people know what they're doing.

I reiterate though, this is *your* plan of attack so you can design and mentally rehearse your approach to solving the problem. Once you've done it, walk it through with someone, the workshop owner at least, but preferably also a colleague, especially if you can get hold of another experienced facilitator.

On top of this, I sometimes do a mock-up of what my wall is going to look like. Where am I going to put the different outputs, what size and colour bits of paper or sticky notes will I use?

Coming out of this process, you'll not only be mentally prepared, you'll also know what you need to take with you and what you might need to create in advance.

On the next page is an example of a workshop plan. There's further detail about it in Appendix II. You may not always need this much detail, but I use this when I need to step through the different stages to help me make sure my approach works. I'm one of those kinds of people who use tables. Sometimes it's much simpler, but this is good for those complicated ones with many activities. Often, they won't make much sense to someone else, but they're mainly designed for me.

The outcome of preparation

Poor preparation leads to ineffective workshops. It's as simple as that. Ineffective workshops are tough on your nerves and worse for your reputation. Not having a process to follow will likely cause your workshop to fail unless you're good at thinking on your feet.

Looking at things from the other way around, effective preparation encourages participation. Perhaps the participants have been tasked with some preparation of their own which shows an intention to achieve a result. If they come into a room which is laid out ready with unpopulated charts on the walls, there are tables and chairs laid out in a way which clearly means business, this will also show that you have a structured approach and have put some thought into things. They will see that their time is being valued and will be in a positive frame of mind before you even start. You can see it in their faces as they look around the room and you can feel it in your own confidence.

Agenda item	Process	Deliverable	Length	Ends	Tool / Technique
Welcome and scene setting	• Owner overview • Introductions • Objectives and scope • Workshop agenda • Ground rules	➢ Settled participants	30	0915	Chris presents Role and expertise K K K
Brand and capability	Strategy, brand and message • Company A • Company B • Discuss and clarify • How are we seen? (Industry analyst)	➢ Capabilities ➢ Each company's direction ➢ Perception issues	90	1045	Short presentation to white board Note highlights on flips Note perception issues on flip
BREAK			15	1100	
Opportunities in the market	Each participant: • Briefly state opportunity • What is your reasoning?	➢ Opportunities and evidence	45	1145	Set homework before hand for initial ideas 4 minutes to present
Group the opportunities	• Group the ideas • Name groups	➢ Named groups	15	1200	Six volunteers
Define the propositions 1	Using the groups as a basis • Define proposition • Flesh out • List potential customers • Define business problem • Present back	➢ Propositions	30	1230	Allocate a proposition to a flip and fill in extra detail
LUNCH			45	1315	
Define the propositions 2	Using the groups as a basis • Define proposition • Flesh out • List potential customers • Define business problem	➢ Propositions	90	1445	Allocate a proposition to a flip and fill in extra detail
BREAK			15	1500	

Prioritise ideas	• Reality check
	    • relate to strengths
	    • relate to market needs
		➢ Ideas to focus on
		➢ Parked propositions (not to be taken forward jointly here)
			30	1530	Post-its on 2x2 to prioritise

Next steps	• What needs to happen now? • Who? • Delivery dates?	➢ Action plan	30	1600	Flip chart

An example of one of my workshop plans. The K is for Kevin (me!)

The workshop plan: Key points

- Use interim deliverables to demonstrate progress and manage the risk of running out of time.

- Plan how your outputs will physically be presented.

- Participants' comfort with each other and the process will affect the way they participate at different times during the workshop.

- The agenda is merely a tool to accomplish the objectives. If it turns out to be the wrong tool, make a new one.

- Be careful of over-structuring the workshop and stifling discussion and creativity.

- The more thorough the preparation, the more smoothly the workshop will run.

6

TOOLS AND TECHNIQUES

There are any number of books and websites describing tools and techniques. Below are some common to ones to start you off and give you a flavour. Look for more and vary to avoid going stale.

Group memory

This is the posh name for where you write everything down so that people can see it. Recording things visually is useful because it serves as a memory for the group, but it also means that they can see what you're writing down. If they don't like how you have written what they just said, they are able to tell you.

Whiteboards are found in most meeting rooms and mistakes can be rectified easily. Their downsides are that they are of finite size and if you need to move something, it has to be rewritten. I find them useful for short, informal group work and to have in a larger workshop for the purpose of ad hoc diagrams. The better ones scroll around so that there are a number of pages.

Flipcharts are also common. There is a range in terms of paper quality, varying from cheap paper which lets the ink through onto the page behind (and sometimes the one behind that) to the ones which are giant stickies ready to be stuck on the wall. I use them for recording objectives, issues and actions and when I need a smaller work area than a sheet of brown paper (see below).

Electronic whiteboards are becoming more common and there are an ever changing variety of these as the technology progresses, so this paragraph will soon be out of date. Ones I have used which have electronic pens to draw with have not been very good so far, but the ones which effectively scan the whiteboard and turn it into a digital file can be useful. Others will connect directly to your laptop and these are only going to become better and more flexible.

Brown paper is my favourite because you can make it as big a work area as you need. The downside is that you need to bring it with you and then have the space and type of wall to hang it. This is discussed in more length above (see section on *Room layout* in the **Preparation** chapter). I use it in conjunction with stickies and rarely write on the brown paper itself as that reduces flexibility. Use a tube to protect it when transporting it. If you want a very tidy look, as well as protect the edges, line them with masking tape. If using drawing pins, putting sticky tape on the corners and poking the pin through that will prevent them from tearing the paper.

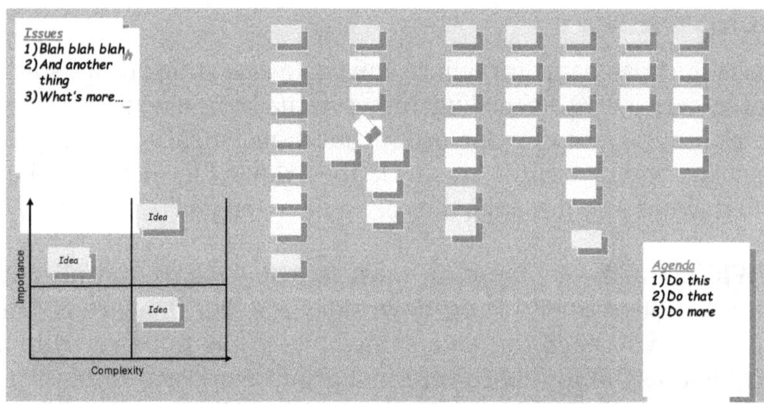

A mock-up of a layout used in planning how stickies will be used.

Stickies were originally invented by 3M and have since been copied by other companies. I use the term stickies generically. I never go anywhere without them because they are so flexible. Outputs can be grouped, moved, removed, re-ordered. There are different colours and shapes which can be used to help codify content. Different brands have differ in quality. Some stay up, others don't.

Brainstorm

The process

I prefer to use the less interesting term idea generation. The reason for this is that brainstorming actually has quite specific rules which I don't always follow.

In a brainstorm you begin by explaining the rules, then you ask for ideas. These are recorded precisely. There is no querying, sorting, discussing or clarifying at all until you finish gathering ideas.

While I sometimes do this, I'll often check I've understood what is meant or avoid putting up a duplicate as I go. To avoid a brainstorm going too wide, start with a question which provides some parameters for an answer.

Either way, the objective is to build on ideas, to have people be stimulated to think of things based on what others come up with and to be free to say what they want, to be creative, to come up with things that they may not otherwise.

Once the group has come up with the ideas, the next step is to make sure everyone understands what's been generated. It may be appropriate to remove duplicates, unless duplicates mean something in your process.

What you do next will depend on why you've generated the ideas in the first place. Often grouping them is next.

Don't under-estimate how many ideas you may get from the group. For example, if twelve people came up with just five ideas each, there would be sixty ideas up there by the end. You'll also need enough space to put all those stickies and a process to use them.

Approaches

There are different ways to gather ideas, the most common of which is all participants calling them out. I usually use stickies to record each idea because they can be easily reused for later parts of the workshop process. It enables me to face the group while I write. It also gives me better control of the pace of ideas coming out: I'm more aware if I've missed any. I can control what is written whereas if someone else writes them down, I would need to keep an eye on them to make sure they're keeping up.

Another way is to a set of stickies to each participant and have them write down their ideas and put them up. This can be useful with a reticent group or individuals or a dominant person who is preventing other ideas from coming out. It also makes sure all ideas are captured.

On the other hand, it means clarification takes longer and there are likely to be more duplicates. Once all ideas are up, it also takes time for everyone to take in what others have written. It is not as effective at stimulating ideas in others. Some facilitators use this to try for some anonymity of contribution. Bear in mind that pen and paper colour, not to mention handwriting, can undermine this.

It can often be used in small workshops or breakout groups where there is the opportunity to explain what is being recorded.

To make sure everyone contributes, you can at least start by going around the table asking for ideas. Inevitably someone will say someone else's idea before you get there. Once this has got going, just let it become free range contributions again.

Brain writing is when an idea is written on a piece of paper which is then passed around the group so that others can add their ideas on the bottom. This can be useful if you want to have multiple brainstorms going on in parallel.

Writing

Some things to consider as you record workshop discussion:

Use more than one flipchart sheet	Avoid cluttering up flipcharts and remember you can use more than one sheet to capture information. Full ones can be removed and stuck on the wall.
Use pens that work	Meeting rooms are full of dying pens. Ditch them and use ones that work. They're much easier to see.
Look out for acronyms	Beware of using acronyms. If there are many, consider building a glossary, visible to all, as you go.
Use pens that can be seen at a distance	Use marker pens rather than ballpoints on stickies so that they are easier to read at a distance.

Avoid writing in red or green	Avoid red and green marker pens on flipcharts and whiteboards. They are low contrast and hard to read from a distance.
Prepare something to stick paper up	To speed up sticking new sheets or paper to the wall, have pre-prepared balls of tack or pre-cut lengths of masking tape on the side of your chart.
Write large enough	Write large enough to be seen by someone with reasonable eyesight. And bigger if at all possible.

Spray mount

Just as stickies use an adhesive which enables them to be moved and still stick, it's possible to buy the glue and effectively create your own. I used to make A5 size stickies and spray each one as I made it. Not only did this go on my tie, but I was probably inhaling too much of it. Then someone suggested the insanely simple idea of spraying the brown paper first.

If you do this, make sure you do it in advance to allow ventilation to remove fumes from the room.

Now you're able to stick anything on the wall and it will amaze your participants. If you used much of it, you may even be able to throw yourself at the wall and stick there.

A word of caution. I have tried a number of different spray mount brands. Some of them simply don't work with the paper falling off again or the fumes are so bad, they're impossible to use. The moral is to try out some before you go into the workshop and keep a stock of the brand you like.

It is also possible to find glue sticks which allow repositioning.

Team sorting

Years ago, when there is a wall full of information to be sorted, for example put into groups or allocated to a chart, I used to do this myself. Then I went to a conference where I saw them make the groups do it. I realised I was being a control freak. I was also boring my participants to death because it is very tedious to watch a facilitator take a sticky and ask the group where to put it when there are dozens of stickies to go through.

As a facilitator, there is already enough to do, so make sure participants do as much of the work as possible. Make them sort it. It will be much faster. You can always review the result afterwards, but it's usually about 80% right. If the group is large, I may ask for volunteers or choose ones myself.

This is also a good excuse to get people out of their chairs and moving. The physical approach stimulates people. It's as if they can actually touch the problem.

Games

Games can be used as ice breakers, energisers or to introduce the subject of the workshop. They can all be combined. Some facilitators use them all the time, others rarely. I use them often when I'm training, but when facilitating, I find the initial brainstorm, for example, can work well as an energiser. What you are aiming to do is to have people be present for the workshop, rather than occupied with whatever it was they had in their minds or were talking about when they arrived.

Ice breakers are there to relax people amongst potential strangers, to act as a leveller and to energise.

I like games with a moral. For example, before a planning workshop, you could have everyone take a blank sheet of paper and a pen or pencil. Make sure the ink will not go through the paper. Have them put the piece of paper on their head. Then ask them to draw a house as you describe it. I like to go back to things they've already drawn, for example asking them to put a chimney on the roof, curtains in the windows or a path leading from the front door.

This is also a useful leveller because everyone looks a bit daft. When you've done, have them take the paper from their heads and admire it. The results are usually amusing and the ones who still manage to get something that looks a bit like a house will be amusingly proud of their work. You can then sum it all up with a moral or punchline such as: "And that's why it's not always a good idea to do anything off the top of your head."

Energisers or warm ups can be used throughout the day. Their purpose is to refresh energy levels and stimulate the mind. They can be as simple as asking everyone to stand up and move around for a minute, they can relate to the topic or they can be a completely unrelated game.

A word of warning: make sure activities are appropriate to the group. Some people love them, others don't. This can be through natural reserve as well as cultural or religious norms. In the case of those who are reserved or consider themselves too serious to be silly, it's amazing what you can persuade people to do if you just get people to do it.

In one team building game which we played with some trainee facilitators in the North East of England, we had them stand in a cluster and each take the hand of a different person in each hand. They then had to disentangle themselves without letting go. The result was amusing to watch and they were successful. The book we found this exercise in observed that we would probably find participants continued holding hands afterwards as they congratulated themselves on their achievement. Our team let go as soon as they'd extricated themselves.

Games can also have some interesting side effects.

We played a game called Name Your Potato, although it can be played with other fruit or vegetables. Everyone is given a potato and their name is written on it. Ask them to close their eyes and to practise recognising the shape of their potato by feel. When they are ready, have them swap with their neighbour so they can feel the difference between the two. Now take all the potatoes and put them on a table. Blindfold each participant in turn and have them find their potato. When we did this, everyone found their potato with ease, except one person. She became upset that she couldn't find it. Some team building exercise, we thought. Then all her colleagues gathered around and consoled her about not being able to find her potato.

Even with national and cultural differences, you can make most games acceptable to most groups if you provide a context and a safe environment for them.

Newspaper articles

This exercise is usually used for imagining a future state. Have groups mock up a media article. Consider the publication in which the article is appearing and provide a headline. Have them provide quotations from stakeholders, relevant statistics, key points such as challenges overcome and reasons for success. There's also room for pictures. The idea isn't to write a full article, but to provide the main information which would form that article.

Voting

I'm always a bit uncomfortable about voting. After all, it's hard enough in a democracy for voting to be fair and to demonstrate the will of all the people, rather than just some of them. So it is in business. And business isn't even a democracy.

Take this scenario.

An organisation is trying to decide between two options, we'll call them A and B. The group is asked to vote on the one they prefer. Option A receives eleven out of twelve votes. Option B receives one vote. The obvious answer is to go for Option A. But what if only that single person actually understands the implications of both A and B?

Of course the implications of both should be properly explained before there is a vote.

Because voting can be problematic, I think that, in general, the result of a vote should be used as the basis for the following discussion rather than a way of actually making the decision.

Segmenting

A further means of segmenting information is through techniques such as SWOT or PEST which provide different lenses or perspectives through which to view the subject.

SWOT stands for Strengths, Weaknesses, Opportunities and Threats. The first two are typically internal to the organisation and the last two external.

PEST stands for Political, Economic, Social and Technical, but you could also add Environmental at least to that list.

You can make up others to suit your needs. They are only prompts to help people think. Another common one is People, Process and Technology, to which you could potentially add Culture and Organisation.

They can also be adapted. For example, SWOT could be altered to be: what you like; what you don't like; what you'd like to be doing; what worries you.

Prioritisation

It is often necessary to prioritise. A commonly used scale is High, Medium and Low. I dislike it because there is no description of what each means and it usually ends up with there being lots of High priority items.

Dai Clegg from Oracle invented the MoSCoW rules, so called because the word forms an acronym. Although originally used to prioritise requirements in agile software development, it can be used in most situations. As with any prioritisation, it helps to avoid wish lists and provides focus on benefit.

Bear in mind that something of one priority may be broken down into components, some of which are a lower priority. For example, it's essential to hang out the washing, but the shirts can wait because you've got plenty of others.

I have provided an explanation in software terms, but these can be adapted for use in other situations.

Must have	Essential to the solution which will not meet the business case or be neither legal nor safe without it. If you can live without it, it's not a *Must*.
	A question that can help decide if something is a *Must* is: "I come to you the night before implementation and tell you there is a problem with a *Must have* requirement and that we can't implement that requirement. Will you stop the implementation?" If the answer is no, then chances are, it is not a *Must have*.
Should have	Separates the sheep from the goats when it comes to "High" priority requirements. Yes, it's important and

> ideally it would be there, but if push comes to shove, the solution could go live without it. There may be a manual workaround or it may become more important in the future.

Could have   Desirable but easier to leave out.

Won't have   Not needed now, or a requirement which has been discussed, then agreed to be left out

A requirement's priority can change as needs evolve. Sometimes a requirement which was once a *Must* decreases in importance when the business realises how much it would cost to implement. They can also change with time. For example, a requirement may be a *Should* until data volumes grow to a certain level, at which point it becomes a *Must*.

Check the business case and priority of objectives for contextual guidance.

Look out for dependencies when assigning a priority. A *Must* cannot depend on a *Should*.

It works for to do lists too. I've used *Must have* when there's a financial or legal consequence such as having my electricity cut off because I haven't paid the bill, or the car being illegal on the road.

Tables and matrices

Structuring and sorting the information you receive can be a large task and tables can help you do this. For example, in a negotiation workshop amongst about ten different banks, I documented the position each bank held on two separate issues in a table. The result showed that there was a disagreement by only one party on each issue, immediately reducing the amount of discussion required.

The two by two matrix is very useful. The X and Y axes each have two values: Low and High, or equivalent. The axes are then labelled according to the required criteria. Examples include:

- Benefit; ease or cost of implementation;
- Impact; likelihood of the event occurring.

Using these is a way to prioritise or focus on what is important according to how the group defines importance. Stickies from earlier in the workshop can be re-used and placed on the chart and the group can place them on the chart themselves and review the result when it is ready. These can be expanded into 3x3 matrices etc if greater granularity is required.

Positives and negatives

There are a variety of different ways of expressing positives and negatives. Each is slightly different in tone so one may suit your situation better than another:

- Benefits and concerns;
- Strengths and weaknesses;
- Advantages and disadvantages;
- Opportunities and threats.

The five whys

Simple root cause analysis. Keep asking why something is the case and you will come to the true cause and therefore the most effective solution. Five whys has come to be accepted as the most you will need to ask.

Where there are multiple reasons, there would need to be several iterations of the Whys to understand the cause of each. Try to avoid sounding like a five year old when using this one.

Group work

They can require more planning, but use these to:

Keep people involved. If you have smaller groups, it's harder for people to drop out or take a back seat.

Manage large numbers. Not everyone is comfortable participating in large groups or perhaps you would not be comfortable facilitating a crowd.

Get more done. They allow for parallel work streams, although each group will still need to feed back on what they did.

Specialise. Specialists can work on what's relevant to them. This avoids potential boredom as well as parallel working.

Isolate participants who may squash other's ideas. Some people, whether by accident or design can prevent others from sharing their suggestions. It may be a boss who is an imposing manager or from a hierarchical organisation; someone who talks a lot which either intimidates the less confident or allows them to not bother; or an expert who either quickly comes down on others' ideas or other participants will defer to because they are assumed to know more or have a better understanding of the topic.

You often won't need a facilitator for each group, especially for a short, simple tasks with a clear purpose. For example: "You have five minutes to come up with all the things that frustrate you. Go!"

Before group work

Explain what each group is doing	Brief the teams before they go into their groups. Make the task as simple as you can to increase focus and reduce the chance of them going astray. There is nothing wrong with a session being only five minutes long.
Allocate a leader if necessary or let them self-select.	If you allocate one, explain their role e.g. to drive discussion, take notes or present back to the larger group.
Give them a timescale	They need to know how long they have. You may include suggestions for how to split up their time.
Provide a format for the output	This can be a description of the required output, a prepared sheet of paper. Where groups were preparing plans they were going to use straight afterwards, I've issued electronic templates and laptops to each group. These can help ensure outputs are consistent and usable for what you're going to do next.

Allocate a facilitator if necessary	Use a facilitator who is not a participant if you have one. Sometimes you may have a dedicated facilitator for each group, at other times there may be a floating facilitator who covers all or some of them.

During group work

Keep on your toes	While you don't need to be on high alert managing a big room discussion, you must still keep tabs on each group and make sure they understand their task and are on track. If you have one or more floating facilitators, they will need to dip into discussions as they find them and provide the odd course correction.
Ensure they are prepared to present back	Ensure each group is prepared to present back e.g. by choosing their three main points.

After group work

Groups report back	Have each group report back to the wider group on what they produced.
Set a time limit for presenting back	If necessary use a timer. Remember that if you let one team overrun, you may need to let the others do so too
Be prepared to facilitate	Be prepared to facilitate a rambling report. Ensure the output is clear and usable.

Some facilitators use groups as their standard way of working. They are avoiding being a control freak and putting power into the hands of their participants. Sure there are disadvantages in this, such as leaving participants to write and structure their outputs can lead to a lack of clarity, but conversely, the fact that they're writing their own outputs increases the level of ownership. You can add a step to clarify outputs if you're worried about it. Just like with anything else, you need to weigh up the advantages and disadvantages.

Tools and techniques: Key points

- Use a flexible medium for your outputs.

- Be prepared for the number of ideas that can come out of idea generation or brainstorms.

- Prepare your workshop materials in advance.

- Energisers can be effective, but they can be inappropriate for some people or situations.

- Use voting to guide debate rather than decide it. The majority is not always right.

- Working in groups needs clear guidelines to ensure each group stays on track.

- Effective sorting techniques can save a great deal of time.

7

STARTING THE WORKSHOP

Set up

Arrive in time to set up the room. Even when you have asked for it to be done in advance, don't rely on this having happened. The tables and chairs may need to be re-arranged. You will also want to put up any brown papers and charts you have brought with you may want to put out name cards.

Familiarise yourself with fire exits and toilets as well as where you will be eating, if not in the workshop room, and where any breakout rooms are, if they've been booked.

Seating

You may want to determine where people sit. If you're expecting there to be different sides in the workshop, they are likely to sit in blocs. Avoid this by providing a seating plan. I was able to avoid this once by scattering the consulting team around the room so that by the time the participants arrived, they had to separate.

Introducing the workshop

There's no particular order to do these and some of them may not be necessary in all workshops.

Warm up: This is an energiser or ice breaking exercise. More on these in the *Games* section in **Tools and techniques**.

Introductions: If some or all people don't know each other, then it's useful for people to introduce themselves. If they all know each other, but you don't know them, then it's also useful as it gives you a chance to find out who they are.

The obvious way to do introductions is to go around the table with people saying their name and something relevant about themselves such as their role, location or particular interest in the project. If appropriate, you can lighten things up by having them add something less relevant such as their favourite food, what they like to do at the weekends or something about them that no one else will know.

Rather than having the creeping death of going around the table, which can lead to people not listening as they worry about what they're going to say, you could pick people randomly or have the last person to speak pick the next person. You can have them toss a ball to the next person.

If you do something different, you can use it as the energiser, but make sure you think it through. If you're random about who goes next for example, it can be hard to remember who's been introduced already and you may not want to appear chaotic right at the start of the workshop.

Use name labels or have cards in front of them. Folded printer paper works well if nothing else is available.

Workshop overview: Sometimes it might be necessary to explain workshops and everyone's role.

Workshop owner kick-off: You've got enough to do as a facilitator, so this is one of those things you're better off handing over to someone else. The background and objectives are going to be much better coming from the workshop owner than they are from you because it's their workshop. Make sure you tell your owner the time you're giving them to speak. It can mess up your plans if you were expecting a five minute introduction and they come armed with 45 minutes of PowerPoint. Especially if you don't have a projector. Actually, if that does happen, I suggest you find out what's in the presentation because its content may mess up your plans, or better still, just ask them then to lose the slides and talk for five minutes.

Workshop objectives: If it hasn't already been stated in the owner's kick-off, clearly explain the objectives, scope and deliverables so everyone is clear on what you're intending to achieve.

Rules

Workshops are a team sport and therefore they need rules. You can either have some prepared or, if you have the time, the participants can come up with them. The latter ensures their buy in, but frankly, unless you have some pretty odd rules, agreement to them shouldn't be a problem.

I once heard a rumour of a website with about 200 workshop rules on it, but I've never been able to find it. Research shows there are only a few rules, but that there are many ways to frame them.

In no particular order, here they are. When introducing them to your participants, it is friendlier to provide explanation of them rather than a simple "thou shalt not..."

The existence of rules does not mean people will always abide by them any more than having speed limits mean that people won't break them. It does however provide a description of the desired behaviour.

Ground rules should be stated at the start of the workshop and then be visibly enforced. Ensure everyone agrees that the rules are reasonable before you start. Use the same rules for all the workshops in the project. People will get used to behaving in the right way.

Mobile phones off

These are a permanent distraction and I'm amazed at how often someone will take a call in a meeting and proceed to have their conversation loudly over the top of the meeting. In these situations, whether I'm running the meeting or not, I have no hesitation in asking that person to leave the room.

Sometimes though, someone needs to have the phone on. They may be expecting an important call which trumps the importance of the workshop e.g. a major incident has occurred which they need to make decisions around or once, a participant's wife was overdue with their baby. In these cases, I ask that they put their phone on vibrate and to leave the room to take the call.

You may also want to extend this to eating, although I often let people finish their lunch into the afternoon session. I just request that they don't spit crumbs at me when talking.

Someone had bought a pie at lunchtime which they brought with them into an afternoon workshop. It was wrapped in a bag made of paper and cellophane. It made a terrible, loud, crinkly crackling sound as he opened it, so the participant tried to do it slowly so as to avoid disturbing everyone. This just meant the sound went on much longer than if he'd just ripped the bag open. I was struggling to hear or concentrate on what the speaker across the room from Pie Man was saying. Meanwhile Pie Man was looking uncomfortable, but his hunger was clearly stronger than his discomfort. Eventually I turned on him and said: "Did you have to buy the noisiest pie in the world for your lunch?"

Everyone laughed, any tension vanished, Pie Man retained his dignity because I had not actually told him off *and* he ripped the pie packet open quickly and finally got to eat his pie.

One conversation at a time

If you allow more than one conversation at time, no one in the room can keep track of them all. Including you. I've seen this worded as "One speaker at a time", but this is actually quite difficult to enforce. People naturally talk over each other in conversation and you only need to intervene if it is an interruption which prevents the first speaker from finishing what they were going to say.

I once had a participant who was deaf. He had brought two signers with him; one would rest while the other was signing. They asked me if I could make sure that only one person spoke at a time because it was difficult to sign when people talked over each other. This wasn't a problem for the hearing participants. I did my best to control this, but it showed just how hard it is for people to really wait until there is complete silence before they start. It was down to the participants to alter their behaviour, which they did as best they could.

Participate actively and share information

For a workshop to be effective, participants need to participate. It's why they're called participants. Everyone has been invited because their input is valued by someone in the organisation. This is the participants' opportunity to have their say, so suggest they don't squander it.

Given this, it is important that people share what they know and be clear where they are less than certain of a particular piece of information. I'll describe how one strength of a workshop is that it is a group building on each other's ideas, so it's okay to only have the start of an idea because someone else may have the rest.

This also leads on to the idea that everyone's input has value and this should be stressed in organisations which are very hierarchical in the way they let people think.

A related rule to this is "Silence is consent", in other words, if you're not saying you disagree, we're going to assume you're agreeing. You can use this in specific circumstances, but sometimes silence is merely that. People need time to think. This is an example of using a rule which expresses the desired behaviour instead of the behaviour which is not required. I prefer "participate actively" because it's clearer.

Respect each other's opinions

Remind your participants that respecting another's opinion is not the same as agreeing with it. It is about giving them the right to a different point of view. If you disagree with it, then you can have a discussion about it, so this rule links directly with *Focus on issues not people* below.

You can extend this by asking people to listen actively. Many arguments come out of people assuming they know what another person is saying rather than actually listening to them.

Related to this is the rule about all opinions having equal value. You may wish to explicitly state this one.

Speak from your own experience

It's very easy to speak for other people or to speak in generalisations and without evidence. So encourage people to use "I" rather than "we", "they" or "you". Stop people from putting their own spin on someone else's story or experience, but let them share their own.

Focus on issues not people

Debate is very much encouraged but should be about subject matter, not individuals. Pounce on this one instantly if you see it happening and reframe the comment (see chapter on **Challenging behaviour**).

Provide explanations – whether offering ideas or disagreeing

Each participant needs to provide explanations of their ideas. This makes for an informed discussion and promotes reasoned debate. You can't just tell someone their idea is rubbish. Instead, talk through your concerns or, better still, ask challenging, yet respectful, questions. Then you've got something to talk about. The whole point is to increase understanding of another's point of view.

Issues are parked

An essential tool in the workshop is the Actions and Issues List, Car Park or Parking Lot (or even Fridge). This is used to note discussion points which need not take up workshop time.

Tell participants that you're not going to just let them ramble on for hours not getting anywhere.

Items on this list may be:

Actions: Where something needs to be done outside the workshop, note it down. This can stop conversation going on unnecessarily when the point can, and indeed should, be dealt with outside the workshop. In other cases, you may not have either the information or participants to deal with the issue.

Circular conversations: This is where the discussion cannot move on because, for example, the information is not available. Sometimes these resolve themselves naturally later in the workshop or the information can be obtained during a break.

Off topic: It is almost inevitable that discussion will stray beyond the defined scope. In some cases, noting the point can make it easier to move on. It may well become an action item.

Note each down and assign an owner and a date, if required, so that it becomes an action. Be clear to participants that you have done this. This is particularly important to the person who made the point.

Make sure all issues are fully worded. I've seen these noted down in a word or two and even as soon as the end of the workshop everyone has forgotten what it was about.

If you don't understand what it is, ask the participant who brought it up to word it for you.

Be on time

You need to model this by starting each session on time. Some organisations seem to have a culture of starting meetings five or ten minutes later than their scheduled start time. This is self-perpetuating because people won't show up to a meeting at 10am if they know it won't start until 10.10am. State on the invitation that you are serious about the start time. I once ran a series of workshops at a company where this was the case. I started my first one when I said I would (although covered relatively expendable items such as introductions) and people came on time to the next.

No war stories

Everyone loves telling stories, but they take up time. If the story is useful, make sure you have the teller extract the moral of their tale. For example, if someone is in a business continuity planning workshop and they're talking about the time their office was flooded and everyone had to go home, you could ask them to describe the impacts on their business so you can start extracting some scenarios for people to talk about.

If it's not relevant, then you need to stop them so you can continue the workshop. Try saying something like "That sounds like a great story, make sure you tell us over lunch." This is an example of telling someone to shut up without saying shut up.

Have fun

I rarely say this explicitly, but I do try to make my workshops an enjoyable experience. In fact I try to do this with all work. My aim is to do a good job first, and to have fun while doing it. It's only work after all. If people are having fun, they're also less likely to have an argument, they'll be more relaxed and do better thinking.

Workshop specific rules

You may require extra rules to suit your particular workshop. These could include ones around confidentiality and diversity.

How to present the rules

Always talk through your ground rules at the start of the workshop. Check that everyone understands them and is prepared to go along with them. You could stick up a poster containing the rules as a permanent reminder of them. Whatever you do, you need to make them real by enforcing them if participants break any of the rules. Ways of doing this are listed in the chapter **Challenging situations**.

> A hotel meeting room had a large wardrobe on one side of the room. When I'd finished talking through the rules, I joked that anyone who disobeyed them would be put in the wardrobe. One of the most senior managers in the room immediately stood up, went over to the wardrobe and climbed inside.

One morning, as I was dropping my son off at school, I noticed a set of rules on the door describing how everyone was expected to behave. I was struck by how similar they were to the ones I use in my workshops. I'll leave it to you to ponder what that may tell us about children and adults.

- One person talks at a time
- Put your hand up if you want to share something
- Listen to Mrs Perelini
- Be friends
- Sharing is caring

- Put things away when you have finished
- Walk
- Keep hands and feet to ourselves
- Have fun!

Starting off: Key points

- Ensure you take enough time to introduce the workshop. It sets the right tone and everyone will begin from the right place.

- Rules set the expectations for the tone of the workshop.

- Rules can be listed, presented and made up by participants.

- For a workshop to be effective, participants need to participate.

8

FACILITATING THE WORKSHOP

So, you've done your preparation and the day of the workshop has arrived. This is where you realise that the facilitator is like a swan on a lake. On the surface, everything looks calm and ordered, but under the water, the feet are going like the clappers as you:

- Keep an eye on the time and where you are in the agenda;
- Try to understand what people are talking about;
- Summarise where required;
- Ensure specific participants are involved where you think they will have an opinion;
- Work out whether a conversation is going somewhere and if it is not, move it along;
- Keep an eye on whether discussion is going beyond the workshop's stated objectives;
- Challenge the group if you think they are not dealing with a topic sufficiently;
- Listen to what's being said and clarify where you don't understand: it's much easier to exercise control if you're listening;
- Maintain neutrality and manage behaviour;
- Record the outcomes.

Maintaining control

As facilitator, you control the workshop. For their part, participants cede control to you so that they get done what they need to do. It's their problem, not yours.

You decide when it's time to move on, although you may ask for the participants' opinion; you give permission for someone to draw a picture; you let people come out and group stickies and then tell them when it's time for them to return to their seats.

This is important. It is liberating for the participants to know that they can be free to think and talk, knowing that the facilitator will reign them in if it's not relevant and tell them what they're going to do next without them having to think about it.

Setting the tone

There can be a particular tone which the facilitator may adopt depending on the type of workshop or even the stage it's in.

When finding and gathering information, you'll need to be open and inclusive, careful of involving everyone whether they appear to have something to add or not. Those who have provided input are more likely to feel they have a stake in the output. This type of workshop usually happens early on in a longer process, so it's vital that the ground can be covered with as few gaps as possible.

With decision-making and negotiation, you need to achieve consensus. You'll need to carefully work through disagreements. The workshop will need to be structured, inclusive and thorough, ensuring all options are explored appropriately. You'll also need to create an environment where participants feel it is safe to change their mind. They can do this if options are analysed carefully and are clarified so that decision-makers are effectively given new information which enable them to revisit existing positions.

When facilitating a workshop to record reactions, such as a retrospective, options analysis, prototype or assessment, you'll need to ensure balance in the reaction: not all good and not all bad either.

Adopting a style

I find most people have a style of facilitating which is linked to their personality. Think about how your style comes across and what it's advantages and disadvantages are. Here are three examples to show you what I mean.

The jokey style: Keeps things fun, people enjoy themselves while they work and it's even less appropriate to pick a fight with someone. If taken too far, the downside could be that people may be having so much fun they forget to work, or your customer may not think you're taking the job or their input seriously.

The business-like style: Brisk and upbeat, you move the workshop along nicely, providing energy which keeps the group awake and on their toes. Take this too far though and you don't give people time to think as you move them along at too fast a rate.

The laid back style: Calm and calming, people have time to think and it takes effort from participants to become over-excited. But you can be so sedate that energy dissipates and people fall asleep or that the pace slows down so much that you're unable to get through everything you had planned.

The best approach of course is to vary your tone throughout the workshop, judging what is required at any given point.

The personality of your participants will also have an effect.

I like to keep things light and jokey, but I once had a workshop where every attempt at humour failed. They seemed to take life very seriously and work was clearly a solemn business. I realise not everyone gets my sense of humour, but most participants make jokes themselves. Not in this one. They remained stern throughout and it felt like one of the longest workshops I've ever facilitated.

Whatever your style, keep it your own and be yourself. You may see another facilitator's style and try to take it on, but if it's not a natural fit, it's going to be uncomfortable both for you and your participants. If you're the kind of person who can't make a joke to save their life, don't try to crack any. There's nothing so horrible as the tumbleweed-blowing-across-the-desert silence that comes with a joke no one thought was funny.

Neutrality

As facilitator, you should be neutral, that is to say, you don't have a stake in the workshop's outcome. I've come across many business analysts who need to run requirements gathering workshops but who are concerned that they aren't neutral. This should not be a problem if you consider that they are neutral in the sense that the requirements aren't their own.

Being neutral helps you to facilitate. It means that you don't get involved in the debate within the workshop. If you did, there would be no one facilitating. Alternatively, participants would see that you were no longer impartial and you would lose some, if not all, of your ability to manage the discussion. It's not for nothing that the referee at a football match doesn't also try to score goals.

I've seen what can happen when the facilitator enters the debate and things start to spiral out of control very quickly. If you are facilitating many workshops for a single project, as you become more involved in it, you can start forming your own opinions and wanting to challenge participants. You need to be careful about how you do this.

The safest way to involve yourself in discussion is to ask questions. For example, if you think a team is making a plan which does not take into account something which you believe is important, how do you raise it?

You could say, for example: "You need to include much more time for testing than that."

But they might respond: "No, that's plenty. What do you know?"

On the other hand, you could try: "Let's just check we've thought about the different types of testing which need to be included..." In this case, you're inviting them to think through the steps themselves so that they can come to their own conclusions.

Another approach could be: "Bob, didn't you mention earlier that there would need to be a large amount of regression testing if this approach was taken?"

Here, you are prodding Bob to make the challenge for you based on the expertise he presumably has.

In both cases, you have raised a point for the participants to work through themselves. You still remain outside the discussion and able to manage it.

These are just two examples, but there will be others that you could find for your particular workshop.

If a group has become stuck and is unable to move itself forward, you can try summing up where you think they have come to: "What I'm hearing is... " Then let them correct you, but use it to show what has been agreed so far and so move them forward when they thought they were going nowhere.

Alternatively, you can say "How about this as an idea?" and then invite them to shoot down your idea and rebuild it.

As a last resort, if you happen to be an expert in the area they are discussing and you believe they are plain wrong, there is one final approach you can take. It is risky and you must do it with great care.

Explain that you have something to contribute and are going to take off your facilitator hat while you do so. Explain why you are going to contribute and any credentials you have. Make your contribution, ensure it is understood and then, very clearly, return to your role of facilitator.

You need to realise that if there has been any discussion while you are contributing, facilitating it will be difficult as you have, however briefly, become a participant. Realise also that no matter how clearly you think you have demarcated your facilitation and participation, participants may now be confused about your role.

Ideally, if you realise this is likely to happen in the workshop, perhaps you should be a participant and someone else should facilitate it.

Neutrality can be difficult to prove. I have often been in a situation where I am a facilitator from a vendor organisation running a workshop between that same vendor and one of their customers. In these cases, the customer would be justified in suspecting that I will run the workshop in a way which favours the vendor. The way around this is simply to prove otherwise. Intervene, challenge and seek clarity in the same way for each party.

A customer asked one of the vendor experts a question. The participant gave a vague response which did not answer the customer's concern. I waited for the customer to pick up on this, but they did not, simply letting it go for whatever reason. So I challenged the vendor participant to answer it properly. It quickly transpired that he did not have the necessary information. He was clearly uncomfortable and indeed embarrassed by not knowing the answer. I registered an action to provide the answer and we moved on. In doing this I was making the problem about the information not being known rather than the evasive behaviour of the individual. Despite that, I had a chat with him after the workshop to apologise for putting him on the spot and to explain why I had done it.

Observing

You need to watch everyone in the workshop. Are they involved? Who's chatting to their neighbour or checking their phone. Who's doodling? Who's engaged? What emotions are they showing? Who clearly has something to add, but is waiting for a lull?

Clarifying

Ensuring everyone understands what is being said in the way the speaker meant it is central to the facilitator's role and something which new facilitators often struggle to do consistently. To do this, you need to be:

- looking for potential alternative interpretations or lack of clarity in what is being said;
- on the alert for a response from someone that suggests a misunderstanding, sometimes shown by anger or frustration or simply talking at cross purposes;
- thinking of implications of what is said;
- looking for a lack of consistency in reasoning or points of view;
- looking for clues that show different basic assumptions are being made.

If this occurs, you will need to check your understanding. Ask questions to clarify. Try to be aware of where assumptions and inferences are being made and test them.

Sometimes participants will assume they know what the other is saying and fail to listen to what is actually being said. This can be very clear to the other participants. It is always amusing, and a relief, when you're able to say to two increasingly flustered participants: "I think you're agreeing with each other." Often the other participants will chorus "YES!" You then need to reiterate what each is saying.

Be aware of apparently innocuous words which are loaded with meaning in the participants' world. Once I was describing how an application was being assessed and several participants kept correcting me. I realised that "assess" to them meant a specific kind of assessment when I was using the word generically. Another participant solved the problem by suggesting I use the word "check" instead. I did and everyone relaxed again. The simple moral is that words are important and can mean different things to different people. Even if you say you are using the word in a different way, many participants will simply not accept it. If this is happening, use a different word.

Reflecting

Repeating back to someone is useful for a number of reasons. It can repeat an important point; it can get them to hear it for themselves and potentially modify it, for example if it was a gross generalisation; it can give you time to think.

Summarising

This can be used as another form of reflecting, but it is useful in other ways. It checks understanding because the person you are summarising has the opportunity to modify your summary. It shows that you're listening, which is you modelling appropriate behaviour, and gets people on side. Most important perhaps, it helps everyone else understand what has just been said.

People often think while they are speaking. This means that they are working out the point they want to make at the same time as they're making that point. This often results in a lengthy answer in which the point is not as clear as it could be. Your summary can make that point clearly so that it is not lost on other participants. If you're going to record that point, it helps you get to the nub of it.

Interpreting

If you or any participant speaks on behalf of another participant, always check back with that person. Often this is useful where someone is struggling to make their point clearly. It can often go along the lines of: "What I think Dana is trying to say – and Dana, tell me if I'm wrong here..." Make sure you don't interrupt them when you do this.

Watch out for people putting their own spin on a comment, whether deliberately or accidentally.

Challenging

As I've mentioned above, this is a way of raising points which you think have been missed by the group. Raise the challenge and let the group then discuss it.

You might also want to suggest something that others can build on or knock down and rebuild in a better way. You may be devil's advocate, being deliberately controversial to provoke a reaction. It is often a good idea to make it clear that you are doing this to avoid any misunderstandings of your role or intelligence.

Checking progress

How much time have you left and how far through the agenda are you? How much further discussion does the group think they need to have around a given topic?

Be aware that a group will often speed up on tasks as they become more used to them. I have had workshops where I've needed to define and understand, say, ten different processes. The first takes most of the morning, leaving me little more than the afternoon to cover all of the others. This has not been a problem though because the first was the central one and had a number of variations to it. The others are supporting processes which are much simpler to work through and everyone now has a working understanding of how I want to define them.

On the other hand, you may be pondering which parts of the agenda you can cut or even drop if required or whether you can shorten lunch. You may keep these decisions to yourself or give the group the choice as to the course of action. Ultimately it's their workshop and they may prefer to have the chance to talk about B rather than continue with A.

Problem solving

This is not about solving the problem which the workshop was convened to resolve. This is how to deal with an apparent shortage of time, why the group seems lost, why your process isn't working and how you're going to stop that person over there from exploding with rage... See the next section.

Crisis intervention

Ah yes, the crisis. There are several types: the fire in the building, the completely failing process, the workshop kit that never shows up. But here I'm talking about the people variety, the ones in which you can intervene.

The best way to intervene in a crisis is for it never to have arisen in the first place. I'm not just being smart, it's what you're doing as a facilitator. I've already talked about being warned beforehand about participants only to find they are model participants. I suspect this is because they can see they're going to finally get a chance to speak. People become upset when they're frustrated, shut down, ignored, insulted. They can also become upset when they're tired or have just received some bad news.

So you can avoid crises by establishing a respectful, listening environment and a robust process that accepts and analyses all points of view.

If preventing the crisis is not possible, the next option is to nip it in the bud.

An operational team was defining requirements for a new system. I noticed that one of them would make needling comments aimed at one of his colleagues. She was rising to each one of them. It appeared to be part of their, somewhat dysfunctional, work relationship. She was irritated, but it hadn't turned into anything more than that yet.

I didn't like it. Not wanting to address it in front of the whole group, I waited until a break then took the man to one side. I told him that I didn't care what he did in the office, but what he was doing was causing problems for the workshop. I asked him to stop. He did - at least for the duration of the workshop.

Here's a similar example:

Participants at a project retrospective were discussing things which had not worked so well. One had not been involved in the project so far, but was about to take over Phase 2. As he heard some of the tales of woe, he would shake his head in disbelief and make disparaging comments. He may have been right to be surprised, but he had the advantages of both objectivity and hindsight and he was undermining the safe, open environment.

Once again, I used a break to deal with him. People are much more reasonable when you get them on their own than when they're in front of other people. The need to save face is probably universal.

I explained to him what I had observed and what I judged its effect to be. While I sympathised with his views, I asked him to desist. He understood what I was saying and I had no more trouble from him.

And sometimes the bud nips itself...

Some senior management peers were in a workshop together. Two of them, who I will describe as Big Gruff Yorkshireman and Energetic Little Bloke, were sat next to each other across a corner.

Big Gruff Yorkshireman made a comment.

"No, no, no, no, no," said Energetic Little Bloke in a very annoying and dismissive way, which made me suspect trouble was about to happen.

I moved forward to stand in the corner closest to them so that I could try to calm any fallout. As it happened, there was none. I suspected they knew each other well and, besides, Big Gruff Yorkshireman had a skin as tough as a rhino and wasn't going to lower himself by rising to such a challenge. I backed off and discussion continued, but my point is, I was ready in case something *had* happened.

Being on the lookout for when you might need to intervene becomes harder the more participants you have. In any single workshop, the following process will loop through your brain many times at high speed. It becomes easier, or at least more habitual, the more you facilitate. No wonder you're tired at the end.

Spot potential problem

First you need to notice something is being said or done which could cause a problem.

Understand behaviour

Next you need to understand why they are behaving in that way, or saying what they are saying.

Decide whether and when to intervene

Decide how disruptive it is, whether it will stop before it becomes a problem or needs to be addressed right then, soon or at a break, or even what would happen if you did nothing. Sometimes intervening might make things worse by drawing attention to something which is about to blow over. It's better to nip something in the bud, but it's not always easy to tell if it will progress into something larger.

Decide how to intervene

Then you need to figure out how to deal with it, which will change depending on the circumstances, people and reason.

Intervene

Finally, if you have decided to do something about it, you need to act. This may include explaining why you are intervening if it helps stop that instance or prevent further examples.

I know that looks like a lot of things to be doing in a matter of seconds, but it gets easier with practice. You're probably already doing much of it as a matter of course in general conversation every day. It's the intensity of analysis and the impact of your actions which is different to normal conversation.

Confronting

I'm not talking about confronting individuals here (As in: "Oi, you, the quiet one! Yes, I'm talking to you. Don't you start going red. Why haven't you said anything yet?") What I mean is where you're confronting behaviour from the whole group.

Examples include them not wanting to talk about what you want them to talk about, or everyone being quiet. This is a sure sign that something is up and you need to understand what it is quickly. I find a direct, honest approach helps here.

"You don't seem to want to talk about this. Am I imagining that or is there something I've done or need to know?"

It's best that you assume you've done something wrong, rather than you assume they're not smart enough to get your approach.

It could be that there's nothing wrong with your approach, but they're a bit tired after lunch or something. In this case there's still something you can do because you can up your energy levels or make a task more interactive. Either way, once you know why a behaviour is occurring, you're in a position to manage it.

Referring

This a great way to win friends and influence people.

"That comes back to the point Raj was making doesn't it?"

"Wouldn't that have an effect on the delivery team? Tony, would you like to comment?"

You're demonstrating you're listening and that you know who people are, but you're also making sure the right people are involved at the right stage of the workshop.

Refocusing

Some workshops are worse than others for this, but everyone needs to be brought back to the topic in hand at some point. While it's good to have some off-topic light relief, if it becomes disruptive, you need to do something about it.

The easiest way to refocus is to pick up the true topic again and keep going without acknowledging the deviation. People usually know when they're off topic and will be accept your subtle refocus.

I have had workshops where I have needed to heavily manage the group and keep pulling them back to the topic. In the worst case, the participants actually thanked me for doing it at the end.

You can even make a joke out of it. Leaping to solutions when you're gathering requirements, especially with solution delivery people in the room is not uncommon. In one workshop, I found a long, pointer resting on the whiteboard. It flexed like an old-fashioned school cane. When I'd had one solution too many, I told the group that I'd cane the next person to talk about solutions. Obviously I'm not advocating corporal punishment for your participants, but the group saw the joke and any tension caused by me closing people down was diffused by the joke of my eyeing them threateningly while flexing the cane.

You might also need to refocus because discussion has strayed beyond the bounds of the workshop's scope or remit. This may result in recording an action to be picked up after that workshop.

I had realised we were entering a discussion that there was no need to have at that point. We had neither the information, nor the participants to have it effectively. It would be dealt with by the project in due course. I interrupted discussion to point this out and there were nods of agreement and acceptance from around the room.

Then someone started up again. She was making the same point, but had been waiting for my interruption to end, so she could make it again.

I waited for her to finish, then reiterated my point, acknowledging hers directly by bringing it into my explanation for why we did not need to have this conversation right then.

Afterwards, a colleague remarked on how he'd found the exchange amusing.

"I wondered how you were going to facilitate it," he said. "You'd just said we didn't need to talk about it. I would have just lost it with her and told her to shut up."

This of course is why he was a project manager and I was the facilitator.

Supporting

Some people are shy, some are quietly spoken or don't feel it's their place to say something. All are just as likely to have something useful to say as anyone else, but you need to get everyone else to listen, sometimes more so.

We probably all know someone who sits quietly in a group and you almost forget she's there amidst all the banter and discussion. Then suddenly she drops in a comment which is right on the money, devastatingly insightful or hilariously funny. In a workshop these people are to be treasured. They're listening, they're analysing and when they say something, it's valuable.

Watch for clues that they want to say something. It will show in their body language. They will be watching the current speaker, they may have their mouth open or be taking a breath as if about to speak.

For the ones who simply speak quietly, the U-shape gives you the means to walk closer to them. They can address their comment to you rather than the whole group and you can provide some amplification by reflecting or summarising the comment.

If someone is interrupted or their comment not addressed, you can ask the interrupter to wait until the first person has finished or make sure that the comment is discussed appropriately.

Energy

Participants will be taking some of their energy from you, so energy and focus from the facilitator is essential. If you feel as though the group has become limp and listless, take a look at yourself as well. Are you getting tired? Are you talking in a monotone? In short, has your energy dropped? This can easily happen because facilitation is mentally draining. If so, step things up a gear.

This could involve talking louder, faster or in a more lively way. It could mean moving the conversation forward or even parking your current discussion because it's going around in circles.

It could also be time for a break. It's up to you how many breaks you take and how long they are. Keep an eye on the time because it can get away from you.

Sometimes, it's only necessary to have everyone stand up and wave their arms and legs about or go for a short walk around the room. Having your workshop plan use group sessions where people need to stand up, move to another part of the room and sit or stand there to do some work for a while is a useful way for keeping people alert.

Listening

It should go without saying that this is fundamental. Have you ever been in a situation when you knew you had someone's full attention, when they were truly listening to you? Think about it now and remember how it felt.

I suspect you felt as though what you were saying was interesting, you felt good about yourself and you warm towards the other person. After all, they thought you were interesting. That's got to endear them to you.

So it is for most people. Listening to others builds relationships. And of course without listening, the participants are not going to understand what is going on in the workshop. Neither will you.

So you need to set an example. The result of not listening is that misunderstandings arise and much conflict arises from even simple misunderstandings.

Listening at that level consistently and constantly is not an easy thing. It takes a great deal of focus, concentration and energy. As we've seen already in this chapter, it's hard to provide that amount of concentration when you consider all the other things you need to do during the workshop.

I generally recommend standing during the whole workshop so that you can move around, maintain a height dominance over seated participants and stay alert. Sometimes however, a discussion is in progress and I feel I can sit down, perhaps merely perching on the edge of a desk. I've noticed the danger in this is that I relax and stop listening. It may not be for long.

So what do you do when your concentration drops? What do you do when you realise you haven't heard what a participant has said, you've even missed a whole discussion? Or perhaps the whole room is now looking at you, waiting for you to respond to a comment or question that you never noticed? As usual, there are a number of strategies you can use.

If it was a single comment that you tuned out on, you could ask them to repeat what was just said, perhaps prefixing it with "I'm sorry, I didn't quite understand what you meant?" Of course, if the question you missed was simple ("When did you say lunch was coming?"), you may look a little silly.

You could also try saying slowly "So...what...you're...saying is........" and hope they interrupt you to say it again anyway and if they don't revert to the one above.

In the end of course, your best policy is honesty. "I'm sorry, I just tuned out a moment there, could you say that again?"

Recovering control

Everyone has their bad days. Just to prove it, here is a description of my worst ever workshop. It shows how you can start off on the wrong foot, then have things spiral against you. It also shows the value of breaks in your workshop as it gave me the opportunity to mentally regroup and more than make up for lost ground.

The company I worked for was running a number of projects for a large customer organisation. The workshop was to put together a closure report on the year's work. As you'll see, I allowed control to slip away from me. I was too distracted by other things to operate correctly. However, my experience gave me the confidence to come back fighting. Things can and do go wrong as they do in any part of your life. Just make sure you learn from them and move on.

Inputs to the workshop were a list of perceived issues. The plan was to agree definitions of the issues and define manifestations of them. We were then to define solutions and actions.

I'd done much preparation. I'd looked at how I would lay out the information on the wall. We had done a dry run workshop and talked through the problem area definitions with two managers. With the benefit of hindsight, it would have helped to have also talked to the real owner, as she turned out to have different views on what we were going to talk about.

On the day of the workshop, I arrived in a bad mood due to bad traffic and a series of infuriating phone calls with customer services, reception and security to try to obtain a car park near the building's entrance so I could carry in all my workshop kit easily. After being passed from pillar to post and having head-spinning bureaucratic conversations, reception wouldn't let me have a car park. They gave the classic reason that someone might need it.

I'd also forgotten to book the room before the workshop so that I could set it up in advance and someone else had booked it already.

My manager, who was present in the workshop and an experienced facilitator himself, reckoned that, being the management team, they'd all be late anyway. As it turned out, they were early.

As it also turned out, it was the wrong room. We were in the much smaller one next door. This was caused by confusing room labelling. One was called 2WS and the other WS2, but I had never looked at both room names before. Frustratingly, the right room had been empty before we went in.

So I started the session by standing in a mountain of brown paper trying to stick some on the wall. I was certainly not in the right frame of mind to run a workshop.

Then irrelevant debate began. It started because one of the problem definitions had mentioned that testing took up 40% of the budget. I'd had an instinctive feeling that using that figure was a bad idea, but hadn't acted on it.

We branched off onto what we should be measuring ourselves against. Both my manager and I suggested this wasn't relevant, but they all seemed to want to talk about it. This included the owner who even went off and got another document. Finally we put that to one side and got through one of the topics we were hoping to talk about.

We were behind, I was a wreck and my credibility was low. Apparently there were mutterings over lunch. To make matters worse, everyone wanted to finish an hour early because they had booked other meetings to go to despite the advertised finish time.

Over lunch, I mentally regrouped and determined I'd be tougher in the afternoon. I tidied up the room so that both it and my head were ready for action.

I began the afternoon by saying we would put the out of scope concerns of the morning to one side and re-iterated our agenda. We were just getting going again when the owner arrived late, said to me – "nothing personal" but the morning had been all over the place and could we agree why we were here and what we were going to do. One of her senior managers kindly explained that we had already been through that before she arrived.

I ruled with an iron rod in the afternoon. I quickly stopped conversations which went off topic, summarised as we went and clearly demonstrated who was in charge of the workshop. What had been missing from the morning was control; I had let their behaviour control me. In the afternoon, I took that control back.

Clear and directive leadership was what this group of people needed. This isn't unusual amongst senior management. I've found that the more senior the participants, the tougher you can facilitate. Perhaps they enjoy the holiday from making decisions.

With my added discipline, we shot through the rest of the agenda and even finished the hour before the scheduled finish time, enabling those who had double-booked other meetings to go to them.

At the end, I received a genuine smile and a thank you from the workshop owner. My manager told me I'd done well.

"Good recovery," he said.

Facilitating the workshop: Key points

- Know your personal style and be true to it.

- The facilitator's job is to provide structure, not to contribute to the discussion.

- It is easier to exercise control if you understand what is being said and remain neutral. Remember the group is the expert.

- Ask questions if you need to contribute, then let the participants come to their own answers.

- Watch behaviour and think about why it is occurring.

- Keep things calm, conversational and respectful so that intense feeling is not allowed to erupt.

- Contributions must be understood. Resistance to a point of view must be respected, provided it is backed up with reasons.

- Involve all participants and direct the flow of conversation; like a traffic cop if necessary.

- Keep discussion moving around the room so that everyone is able to have their say. The softly spoken and inarticulate will need support.

- Avoid doing anything the group can do for itself because you're doing enough already.

- Your energy levels will affect those of the group.

9

CHALLENGING SITUATIONS

We've talked about preparation and getting to grips with the context of the subject matter and process of the workshop, but there's another major consideration when facilitating. The people.

We've already touched on a few situations where participant behaviour leads you to feel the need to intervene. This is part of your role. It is your job to manage debate, encourage contribution and generally see fair play.

People can be the reason for success or failure of the workshop. We've all been in meetings when someone won't stop talking, or wanders off the point or starts recounting war stories and anecdotes. Perhaps the participants know each other too well and their existing relationships make it difficult to work together and reach consensus. This behaviour causes problems and must be managed, but remember when you are managing them that they are just people with their own needs and histories and personalities. They need to be managed effectively but compassionately.

Below, I address a number of types of behaviour. I describe how this behaviour may manifest itself and provide a range of options for ways to deal with it. Some are preventative, others are reactive. They will not fit all situations, but they are tried and tested.

In any given situation, you will need to select the approach which is appropriate to the context and personality of those involved. In each situation, it's important to understand the reason for the behaviour. For example, is someone quiet because they're shy, feel ignored or don't understand what's going on? Knowing that will help determine how you respond.

You may never know why people behave in the way they do, but never assume they are being awkward for the sake of it. Participants are not out to get you (usually). Remember that when you are a participant yourself, you will do things which require the facilitator to manage you.

As has already been discussed, breaks are a useful time to talk to someone. You are not challenging them in public and you can explain the impact their behaviour is having. People are usually reasonable. Of course, if the workshop owner is the problem, you definitely need to talk to them.

Remember, you are not alone. Participants may help you by asking people to be quiet, mediating and digging for information. This will help to share your workload and signal to you that people are comfortable with the environment. You just need to make sure their interventions are constructive and that you do not hand over control to them.

The attacker

A participant offers strong criticism or ridicule of another person, either personally or of their ideas. They may attack the holder of a particular point of view or they may even constantly ridicule a specific person or their ideas. Their manner may be scornful, threatening or abusive.

The danger of this type of behaviour is that it may escalate so that both sides are in conflict and there is no constructive discussion. Alternatively, a less confident personality with important information may be bullied into silence and not share that vital information. This could spread to other participants so that the attacker forces their will on the entire workshop and potentially the project. Some things you can do in this situation are:

Intervene immediately	This needs to happen quickly, before there is any retaliation.
Use your physical presence to break the confrontation	Stand between the antagonists, break their eye contact and give yourself the time to intervene.
Reword to show positive intent	"You didn't phone to say you'd be late because you thought it would make you later."

Keep things conversational so that intense feeling is not allowed to erupt

If the mood is conversational, it's harder for someone to become aggressive. Nightclubs DJ have been known to put slower music if they see trouble brewing on the dancefloor.

Use the power of the group to exert peer pressure on the attacker

The attacker's behaviour will probably make other participants feel uncomfortable or annoyed and the facilitator can use this to the advantage of the process. For example "What does the rest of the group think of that point of view?"

Ask each side to explain why they are holding that position

Ask each side to explain why they hold their position. This explanation may be enough to make the following conversation more reasonable.

Group issues that are related

Related issues can be separate manifestations of the same problem. This reduces the number of issues and with it, potentially, irritation.

State desired behaviour not past complaint

"Don't ask for last minute reviews" is not as clear as "Give at least 48 hours' notice to review a document". Explaining what you want is much clearer than explaining what you don't want, as that still leaves what is wanted open to misinterpretation.

Ask questions focusing on positive aspects of relationships, common vision or success

If a problem is described as "there are misunderstandings with customers when communicating with them", it is potentially misleading. It could be too vague. It may be better, for example, to describe it as "face to face meetings work well, but misunderstandings only occur with business done over the phone" . This is clearer. In this case, misunderstandings become only a symptom of the actual problem.

Ensure they are talking about facts	De-personalise the point that was made and ensure they are talking facts. This may require some reframing.
Identify underlying interests and concerns	What needs do they have? These are what are driving what they are saying.
Find common ground	"You've both expressed concern about the safety of children on the road."

Dominant talkers

People can talk a great deal with the best intentions, or be unaware that they are stifling debate or interrupting others – which is when this is a problem. They may think they are merely taking an active part in the discussion, which is why they were invited; or they may be doing it because they think their point is the most important; or that they are more important than everyone else; or because they don't notice that anyone else wants to speak.

The problem comes when their behaviour stifles the contribution of others. So there are two sides to this problem: one person talking too much while the others aren't talking enough.

Often, the dominant talkers have much to offer. This may be because they know the topic very well and can always be relied on to validate the workshop output as it emerges.

Have a quiet word	Talk to the dominant speaker during the break. They may not realise the effect they are having on others.
Have participants write on stickies	If everyone isn't joining in with a brainstorm, handing out stickies to be completed by participants can provide a means for the quieter members of the group to participate. You can always revert to everyone calling out again once ideas start flowing. This also helps allow for individual differences in the way people participate.

Involve others	Checking for other points of view.
Record their point visibly	Make sure the point being made is visibly recorded. They may have kept going on and on because they didn't feel as if they'd been heard.
Split participants into groups	Encourage others to participate by splitting them into pairs or groups. Someone may be more manageable in a smaller group because they don't feel the need to show-off or because there is someone else in the group who can deal with them.
Casually stand in front of them	If they keep interrupting, as you are moving around the room, casually stand in front with your back to them while focusing your attention on the person who has finally managed to get a word in edgeways. Don't do this for too long, just enough for the other person to start making their point.
Direct conversation away from the person	Involve others by asking them for their opinion. "Hold it a second there Tom..." You can raise your hand a little, but not so much that it's like a policeman directing the traffic which could seem rude in a talk-to-the-hand-because-the-face-ain't-listening kind of way. Then turn your head away from the person and towards others in the group and ask them for comment. It is easier to do this if you have moved towards them. Alternative interruptions include: "thank you", "okay", "we'll come back to that", "hold that thought".
Summarise their points	Then bring others into the conversation by inviting them to contribute.

In a post implementation review, a man had a good deal to say about the new system. He'd even come into work on a day off to make sure he could have his say. Despite being down to earth in his criticisms ("It's a crock of shit."), he also provided specific reasons why he had that opinion. Although his contributions were very useful, he had a tendency to continue making the same point and I found I had to keep cutting him off so that we had time to cover other topics. At the first break of the day, I talked to him to ensure he understood what I was doing, and let him know that I valued his input and didn't have a vendetta against him. He was reasonable and understanding and continued his input without resentment. In fact, he became easier to control as he would remember our discussion when I started to intervene and realise I would only do so if I felt he had made his point.

Off topic discussion

Discussion will naturally go beyond the scope of the workshop or at least beyond where you currently are in the agenda. It may wander completely as someone recounts a story.

Review workshop scope at the beginning	Go over topic and scope at start of workshop to remind them what they are supposed to be discussing.
Record the point as an action to pick up outside the workshop and move on	Just because the point is not in scope, doesn't mean it's not important. You can acknowledge this value by recording it. Explain why you are doing it. This works well if someone keeps bringing up the same off topic comment. They may not realise it is not in scope. Assigning it as an action acknowledges it and shows an intention for dealing with it in the future.
Refer it to the group	Check with the group to see if they feel it needs to be discussed.

Publicise scope before the workshop	Ensure participants know the workshop purpose, including objectives, deliverables and scope.
Pay attention because it changes everything	In **The workshop plan**, I describe a time when the participants insisted on talking off topic and it turned out that they were flagging that the business was about to collapse, which was more important than the workshop's stated objective. In this case, it was clear because all the participants were doing the same thing. If it is a lone voice, it may not be so obvious, but could be as relevant.

Multiple conversations

Sometimes enthusiasm reaches such a point that everyone starts talking at once. Alternatively, it might be a side conversation, sometimes related to the workshop, sometimes not. We're all guilty of that one.

Ignore it	If it's a short comment, let it go. If it begins to distract anyone, especially you, stop it.
Move towards them – like a teacher	If it is just one pair talking, move closer to them, make eye contact or gesture to them to be quiet. Simply moving closer often works as they see you coming and realise why. Where the same two people have often been caught chatting, I've threatened to separate them in a mock teacher voice. I should note that I felt I could get away with this because of how I had judged their personalities and the jokey tone I had already set in the workshop.

Enforce turn taking

You'll get to them in due course. You may need to raise your voice and point out that everyone is talking at once, perhaps adding something about being glad everyone is so enthusiastic.

Point out their input will not be noticed

Draw attention to the fact that their information is neither being heard by everyone nor recorded by you. Tell them you come back to them shortly.

A participant fired up his laptop and chatted to his neighbour about some of the files on it.
"Are you looking for a file for this workshop?" I asked.
"No," he said.
"Could you put it away then please."
It was quick, it worked and it stopped distracting everyone else. I made sure I continued to involve him.

Quiet

This can range from one quiet person to the whole room being quiet. I think many new facilitators think needing to intervene in conflict is the most intimidating situation to deal with, but a room full of quiet people is more common and harder. At least with conflict, you have something specific to get your teeth into.

As with anything, there will be a reason for the behaviour which will determine how you deal with it. Watch body language. Someone can be attentive or they can be disengaged. I would suggest someone who is clearly listening, but has not said anything, is unlikely to be a problem. Don't assume someone who is doodling is not listening.

They may also be quiet because they don't think their contribution is important or withhold useful information for some other reason e.g. not buying into the workshop or wider project; or not realising this is the best time to contribute.

Use energisers

Use icebreaker energisers. See Games section in **Tools and techniques**.

Avoid asking them direct questions	If they seem shy, don't ask them to participate unless you've been doing it with everyone else or they may feel picked on.
Talk to them during the break	Find out why they have dropped out or have not said anything. It could be they are bored, they are shy, they feel they shouldn't be there, they're deliberately attracting attention, or because you or someone else has offended them e.g. by closing them down when they were making a point.
Acknowledge the group is quiet	If the whole group is quiet, acknowledge it and try to understand what is creating the potential disengagement.
Change your process	Change the process you are using to involve them more.
Encourage them with a question	Ask them a question to encourage their participation, perhaps on a subject close to their heart or related to their work area.
Get group members to work on their own	Suggest the group writes down some ideas (e.g. their top 3). Give them a couple of minutes. You can further encourage them by having them discuss their thoughts with their neighbour. Now, suitably warmed up, ask them to share their ideas with the wider group.
Involve them in group activities	Get them involved in group activities, perhaps giving them a specific role.
Allow them to leave	If the quiet person is not relevant to the workshop, get the owner's permission for them to leave.

Broken record

This person keeps bringing up the same point over and over again and tries to focus discussion on this one issue.

Listen and acknowledge	The broken record needs to be heard, so listen and acknowledge their point.
Record the point being made or park it	If it is relevant, talk about it and record the outcome. If it is not relevant, let the group agree that and record it as an issue. Either way it has now been discussed and recorded for reference if they raise it again.
Challenge them to explain why they keep talking about it	If they feel there is still an outstanding issue, ask them to be specific, otherwise get their acknowledgement that the subject has been dealt with or noted. This agreement makes it hard for them to go on.

Negative, sceptical and critical

It's healthy to disagree, but it becomes a problem when it appears to be either a habit or no reasoning is provided which supports this opposite view. Some people seem to always see problems. These are the Won't Work people rather than the Can Do people.

People who won't change are expressing a specific kind of negativity, for example the person who focuses on the way things have always been done. "I've always done it like that and I don't see why I should change." Some people may need to realise it's change or die. Others the group may need to persuade. Others may actually have a point the group needs to understand.

One of the benefits of workshops is buy-in and common understanding. To achieve this, you need all the issues to be out in the open so they can be discussed.

Acknowledge past issues	Sometimes all they are after is that other participants realise there have been problems.

Ask what it would take to change their mind	Try to turn the negative attitude into productive ideas by asking what their concerns are and what it would take to make them happy. If there really are obstacles, they're now out in the open and can be discussed.
Have them suggest a solution	It could be they just do not like the solution being offered.
Use the workshop owner	Use the workshop owner to deliver a 'get over it' message. Sometimes the problem can't be fixed and the person simply needs to move on. This may be better coming from their peers, rather than management.
Imagine the future	Get them to imagine a perfect future scenario and then think about how to get there from where they are now.
Give the participant the opportunity to vent	Once they have done that, try to get them to look forward not backward. On occasion, I've set aside a particular part of the workshop for participants to let off steam.
Involve other participants	Encourage other participants to sell the alternative to them.
Have them explain themselves	Get them to explain so that everyone can understand their reasoning.
Have a separate step for criticism of ideas	You may be able to deal with this with your agenda by separating idea generation from idea evaluation.
Listen to them	Each statement must be understood and credit given where it is due. Resistance to a point of view must be respected, provided it is backed up with reasons. They may be right.

The takeover bid

Participants will sometimes suggest how you should approach part, or even all of the workshop. Usually this happens out of sheer helpfulness. Only occasionally, is it someone attempting to undermine you.

Listen to the suggestion and decide what to do with it

Some comments may be useful. While I've often taken on a suggestion and run with it, be careful of taking on a new method without thinking it through. You've prepared your workshop process with great thought. Make sure the suggestion fits with the rest of your workshop or that it will work practically. If you take it on, you're the one who will need to make it work and will be left looking silly if it doesn't.

Pulling rank

"I've been a project manager for 30 years and I've never done it like that." Yes, you know this person, the one who uses credentials such as age or company seniority to emphasise a point they are making.

Make them justify themselves

We need their reasoning, not just their opinion, so direct questions to that end. "Why won't it work? What is better about your alternative?" Their reasoning can then be discussed like anyone else's.

A discussion was going on and I was just thinking it had gone on long enough and I needed to move it along. Then one of the participants made a gesture to me. Now, I had only been facilitating for a few years. This guy claimed he had been facilitating for a long time. The gesture he made was a 'move this along' signal, rotating his forefingers around each other.

Now that he had made this signal, I was in a quandary. If I moved it along, he would think I had only done it because I had taken his wise advice, and I already thought he was rather smug. If I ignored it, he would think I was a fool because the discussion needed moving along. What to do? Even then, I realised it was the pride of youth in the face of experience which was causing my problem. I swallowed it and moved the discussion along. It was only afterwards that I thought of what I could have done. I should have moved it along and then turned to him and said. "Sorry, what were you trying to tell me?"

The pitch invasion

Someone stands up and starts talking. Where this has happened to me, they've drawn a picture on a whiteboard or pointed at something on the wall. A picture can be enormously helpful; let them get up and draw it. Similarly, pointing at something on the wall is not a problem in itself. The problem comes when they don't sit down again and proceed to run the discussion. This potentially takes control away from you.

Let them do it	It's usually helpful and they will sit down on their own.
Ask them to sit down	Thank them and ask them to sit down.
Direct attention away from them	Move away from them so that eyes follow you, then continue to run the discussion. This will hopefully leave them standing alone and they will sit down.
Leave them talking there for a while	Let them run the conversation for a while, but be careful because you may never regain control again.

I was running a workshop for the wider business unit to which I belonged. The manager, who I did not know very well, was a tall, broad man with a dominant personality. I asked him if he would say a few words to introduce the workshop. He came and stood out the front to do so.

"Who's timekeeping?" he asked after his opening comments.

"That's my job," I said.

He nodded. "Right then, let's do introductions," he said.

I had been about to do that myself, but I let it go. Part way through the introductions, he went and got his chair, put it at the front and sat down. Now I was worried. His personality was as large as his physique; I needed to shift him back amongst the participants or I would struggle with him for control of the discussion.

I hadn't had a chance to even introduce myself yet. As the round the table introductions reached me, I said: "And my name's Kevin Barron and I'm the facilitator, which means I'm the only one allowed up here, so Ian, could you take your chair and sit back down there please?"

I'd said it with a smile on my face and to my enormous relief, he did as I had suggested and everyone had a bit of a chuckle at the same time. Of course what I should have done was brief him before on the format of a workshop, what I expected of him and what I was there to do.

Late arrivals, unexpected participants and early leavers

For the late arriver, I'm talking about the person who persistently arrives late for each session and makes a show of it rather than someone who has arrived late because of traffic or a late train. They may well try to insist on catching up and try to stop the rest of the group mid-stream or try to re-visit decisions which have already been made.

Then there are people who are just so much more important than the rest of us. They can't turn their phone off, they have to keep ducking in and out of the workshop to check on things, sometimes making a big fuss when they do. We'll make exceptions for some people: the man whose wife is about to give birth can leave his phone on; the critical support guy who can only come if he can be easily extracted again. Others are just attention seekers.

Start when you said you would	Enforce punctuality as a ground rule. This is best done by simply starting when you said you would so people realise. Many meetings will only start once everyone is there.
Close the door to signal you've started	When you are ready to begin again after a break, close the door to the workshop. If participants are loitering outside chatting or returning late, they will assume you have started – and indeed you might have done – and hopefully will rush to rejoin the discussion.
Use a break	Talk to them during the break if necessary.
Find out before if anyone needs to leave early	Find out before the workshop happens, or at least at the start of it if anyone has a problem with the end time. You may be able to talk them out of it or re-arrange some of the sessions so as to make the most of the time they have.
Ignore them	Treat the person who comes and goes as if they are continually arriving late. Don't go back over things they missed, discourage them from leaving, ignore the fuss they make if they do.
Provide some brief context	If someone is late just the once, you may feel it is appropriate to give them some kind of brief context, e.g. "We're just talking about the risks."
Don't stop early	Do not stop the workshop for early leavers unless they are vital.
Welcome them, but do not backtrack	Welcome the latecomer, but do not disturb the workshop to summarise for the late-comer's benefit.
Use music	Music can be a low-key way of

warning that you're about to start again and that they should come back.

Delay the start a little — For latecomers, delay starting, but not by much. Check to see if others know whether they are definitely coming.

Changing goalposts

This can happen because the owner or participants want to talk about something else, or because an issue has come up which means the original objectives are no longer valid. An example of this is above in the chapter on **The workshop plan**.

Redefine the scope and quickly re-plan — Redefine the problem or reduce the scope. You may see what you need to do, but participants may still use original objectives, scope and deliverables. Make it clear these have changed.

Take a break — Stop and take a break to assess the impact and decide a course of action.

Ask the owner — Talk to the owner or take stock with the group about what to do.

Participants intimidated by more senior participants

Participants might say little or nothing, or sometimes all heads turn to look at the senior person when a question is asked.

Have the owner state everyone's views are equal — Have the workshop owner say up front that there is no rank within the workshop and that all ideas will be treated on their own merits. This won't work on its own, but it's a start. You need to demonstrate this by clearly enforcing the rule as well.

Use a levelling game	Use a levelling game at the start of the workshop. Sometimes these require everyone to do something silly. It's a bit like imagining someone who intimidates you sitting on the toilet. Without the toilet.
Use break out groups	Remove senior managers who may be inhibiting open discussion e.g. hold sessions in groups where they are kept separate.
Remove the senior people	You could be overt about it by asking the senior people to step out of the workshop for a time, explaining why you are doing so.
Avoid the senior people	Perhaps it would be best to not have those senior people in the room at all or have a completely separate workshop for them. You can be open about your reasoning: that it's the only way they'll get honest opinions.
Quickly deal with anyone who pulls rank	If anyone appears to pull rank, you will need to move swiftly as in dealing with The Attacker above. Participants need to see that you are enforcing the ground rules and providing a safe environment for them to speak. This means dealing with the rank puller, as well as supporting the speaker.
Reiterate why participants were selected	Re-iterate why all participants are there; they have been selected because they have useful knowledge. Have the senior managers do it themselves if necessary and then ensure those managers really do listen, respect and at least sometimes agree with what those more junior in the organisation chart are suggesting.

Talking in foreign languages

In this multi-cultural age, it can happen that there are people in your workshop who have another language in common and can use it to talk to each other without anyone else understanding. This can undermine trust, but it also prevents a full, open discussion.

Let it happen, if brief	Let it happen if it is just an aside. If it keeps going, treat like any other side conversation.
Research cultural norms	When workshops involve other cultures, do some research on customs to avoid potential misunderstandings.
Allow complex discussions if summarised afterwards state the answer	Sometimes participants need to revert to their native language to discuss a complex idea. A ground rule up front could allow for this so long as the result of the discussion is given in the common language.

Despite the customer being German and the supplier being Swedish, the project language was going to be English. Another piece of etiquette was that we needed to address the Germans more formally, for example as Mr Schmidt. We decided we would need to apply this rule to all of us, not just the Germans.

When it came to our first meeting, the Swedes found it hard to remember each other's surnames and would resort to Mr Magnus or Mr Kevin, for example. Our main customer was Dr Wagner. I had been calling him Herr Doktor Wagner. During the morning he came up to me.

"There's no need to call me Herr Doktor Wagner - " he smiled.

After all that, he's going to let me call him Wolfgang, I thought.

" - Herr Wagner is fine," he continued.

Tired participants

Participants are yawning, eyes are drooping and they may even go to sleep. Can be more likely after lunch.

Cool the room	Cool the room down. Open a window.
Speed up	Pick up the pace of the workshop.
Plan or change your agenda to compensate	Be aware that this is more likely to happen after lunch, so ensure what you are doing then is lively. Going into break out groups will get people moving and more involved.
Take a break	Take a short break. This can be as simple as getting participants to stand up and walk around or swing their arms.

Participants' friends

Unexpected people show up, sometimes invited by participants.

Ask them why they are there	Ask them why they are there and what they would be able to add.
Ask them to leave	Either you or the owner should ask them to leave, explaining politely that the plan, the room size and the catering do not allow for extra people.
Let them stay	They could be valid participants who were overlooked during preparation. If your plans allow for it, let them stay.
Ask the owner	Refer to the owner to decide whether they should be allowed to stay.

Remote participant

It is becoming more and more common for participants to be present via teleconference or video link. This makes them harder to manage because they are not around your table and many tricks and techniques can't be used.

Give them airtime	Ensure those present do not talk over the remote participant. It is very easy to make it hard for them to take part.
Ask for specific input	Ask for feedback at regular intervals.
Point their camera at group memory	If it is a video link, ensure the camera is pointed at the group memory.
Use two cameras	Have one camera for participants and another for group memory. Ideally also one screen per camera. Again, ideally, this should be replicated at each location.
Describe what they can't see	Describe things that are happening in the workshop where necessary.
Avoid having any remote participants	Inform participants that being present via telephone is pointless because the work is going to be done visually.

Concern over personal impact

Sometimes during a workshop, a participant can become worried by potential impacts to them e.g. that they may lose their job or have to change it or that it could happen to their colleagues.

Add to issues list	You may not be able to deal with it during the workshop, but it will still need to be addressed.
Understand their concerns	If it's unclear if their unease is due to impact on themselves, you will find yourself dealing with them as the negative, sceptical and critical behaviour above. If they are showing unease, gentle questioning to tease out the issue, potentially in the break, may provide the insight.

Acknowledge their concerns	Acknowledge their concerns and clarify why they are worried.
Refer to the owner	Refer it to the owner who may be able to allay any concerns there or at least provide extra context.

Legitimately distracted

Someone is distracted by an aspect of their job or something happening in their life e.g. they are on-call.

Check beforehand	Ask beforehand or analyse participant list. Try to find out if they are able to divert urgent calls to someone else.
Let them leave	Give them permission to leave or take a call (outside the room) and inform others about circumstances.
Use an external venue to reduce interference	Use external venue which reduces the ability of daily business issues to interfere with the workshop.

A participant was behaving in an irrational and angry manner. Talking to the man during a break, the facilitator discovered that his wife had left him that morning. The facilitator checked with the owner, then sent them out of the workshop. They clearly had other things to do, or at least other things on their mind and it was helping neither the workshop nor them to stay.

Sometimes the distraction is lighter in nature.

I noticed one participant looking at something at floor level.
   "There's a mouse down there," he said.
   "I've already called Facilities," said the project manager, as if to prove he was the project manager.

The mouse continued to sniff and run around in the corner. It was making several participants nervous and everyone else was distracted watching it. After a few minutes, I asked if we should stop the workshop and catch it. Everyone agreed.

I had a long plastic tube for carrying my brown paper. We laid this on the ground. Someone provided a piece of apple and we put it in the mouth of the tube.

Two people from Facilities arrived with a trap containing poisoned bait. None of the participants liked the idea of our mouse being killed like that and we watched as the lady from Facilities placed the trap under the cabinet in which the mouse appeared to have made its home. The two of them left and we carried on. A few minutes later, one of the participants exclaimed that the mouse was in the tube.

We looked and there it was, just inside our tube, not the trap. I crept over, upended the tube and heard the mouse and apple slide down to the bottom. A participant then took the tube outside and let the mouse go. The workshop continued, the mouse lived to see another day.

Participant is sick

A participant is acting in a fidgety manner, looks unwell or leaves the room. They may also tell you they feel unwell.

Check they're okay	Be concerned. Ask if they need help.
Let them leave	Let them get a drink, have a break or even leave. You may send someone to check on them or to escort them.
Obtain input later	Follow-up after the workshop to gather contribution if appropriate.

Unsubstantiated information

This is where a claim is made which impacts the work you are doing or the people involved. For example: "I've heard they're closing the eastern office. How will that affect our planning?"

Debate on the veracity or impact of these kinds of comment can easily take over.

| **Make an assumption** | Make an assumption and move on, you can assume more than one scenario. |
| **Check if anyone knows anything** | Sometimes a participant will know the truth of the matter, otherwise it might just need a quick phone call to resolve. |

Body language

Sometimes a participant won't say something, but may shake their head, frown, look surprised or make noises.

| **Act on the visual cue** | Make their opinion explicit by asking for verbal agreement, disagreement or explanation. Deal with what they say. |

We were discussing how many new file servers would be required to support a major new system. A man from the Operations team pulled a face, but said nothing. I noticed and asked why he had done that. Only then did he tell me that the server room was not large enough to hold that many servers. It is possible he would have taken it upon himself to investigate an alternative, but no one else would have known about it had I not noticed his wordless reaction.

The pedant

There's always someone who will point out that you can't spell (usually it's me). Others love to be mired in detail. It could also be where one party, potentially the facilitator, believes there's a generic structure (e.g. a process model) into which everything fits. The other party believes their case does not fit the model, that it is special.

Use an example to show level of detail	This is much clearer than a long explanation.
Apologise for your spelling up front	If you know spelling is a weakness, apologise up front, make it unnecessary for them to be so clever. Spelling only matters in this context if it impedes understanding.
Focus on the differences	Where someone believes they don't fit the generic model, explore those alleged differences. Talk through specific examples and scenarios.
Halt the flow of information	When someone is getting into too much detail, you need to pull them back. Give them an action to provide the detail later if it's relevant, but not required right then. Otherwise thank them and tell them that they have provided enough.

The joker

Some people just love to make jokes. They are only a problem if they obstruct the objectives of the workshop. They can be useful by keeping the mood light and people happy and they like being the centre of attention so you can use them as the butt of jokes yourself. But they can be too much of a good thing.

Refocus on the topic	If they become obstructive, refocus attention on the agenda and away from them. At this point the joker is behaving like someone who talks too much and doesn't let anyone else speak. Deal with them accordingly.
Use a break	Thank them for bringing in some fun, but explain that you need to keep things moving as well so to tone it.

The secret agent

This is a tough one because it can be hard to even know it's going on. It's where someone doesn't tell you something for whatever reason, yet it's a vital piece of information. While I've discovered a number of these in the course of the workshop, it's of course possible that others passed me by because they never let on.

Once, I had a participant say "At last we get to the heart of the problem! I wondered when someone was going to bring this up."

Request sharing up front	Make sure that you discuss the ground rule about sharing information and explain why it is important.
Pay close attention to negative or cynical participants	This kind of behaviour often comes from those who don't believe the process will work and so don't fully contribute. Their withholding information may not be malicious; they simply don't see the point in sharing it. So watch for body language or facial expressions that show a reaction to discussion you may want to make explicit. Involve them in discussion by using their examples and demonstrate how their scenarios fit.
Demonstrate how valuable the contribution was	Thank the person for the contribution and play up its importance. Demonstrate how you can usefully discuss it. In this way, you are modelling effective use of information and letting the participants decide what is and is not useful to the workshop process. This will hopefully discourage any similar behaviour.

The mule

People can be stubborn. They take positions on a topic with varying degrees of flexibility. Those hardest to deal with close down and refuse to hear what is being said. Even if they appear to be listening, they can actually be filtering everything through prejudices and assumptions and hearing only what they want to hear – and therefore not listening at all.

Say it in a different way	Say it in a different way such as by analogy or step by step. Take them on a journey rather than present them with a destination.
Get someone else to convince them	At other times, a different person may receive a different response, especially if that person is one they respect.

Too many paths

This often happens when working through processes. You find you need to follow the process through e.g. multiple channels (an order comes in by email, phone call etc), or there are a number of alternative paths. It feels overwhelming. How can you do it all?

Do the standard or sunny day first	Often called the "sunny day" scenario, start with the path through the process which is the one where everything goes smoothly. Once that's mapped, it's clearer to see where the alternative paths diverge and ensure you cover them all off.
Pick one	Sometimes you just need to decide which path you will do first. This could be the most common for example. Once you've explored this, pick another and identify any differences to the first. I've often found little or no differences.

Remember to deal with any behaviour with sympathy. After all, one day, *you* could be that participant.

Challenging situations: Key points

- Behaviour only becomes a problem if it's getting in the way of achieving the workshop objectives.

- Understand why someone is behaving in a particular way and how to deal with it becomes much clearer and easier.

- Find a way of shutting people up without saying shut up.

- Reframing a statement is a powerful way of getting an emotion fuelled discussion back on a constructive right track.

- Inside the group, give credit to individuals for an idea. Outside it, give credit to the group for ideas.

- Listen to your instincts.

- Once you know why a behaviour is occurring, you're in a position to do something about it.

10

AFTER THE WORKSHOP

Finishing off the workshop neatly is an opportunity to sum up and tidy up any loose ends. But your role in the workshop may not stop when the workshop has finished. You may be asked to document it or to manage the follow up of actions. Strictly speaking, neither is the role of a facilitator, but it is often the job of the person facilitating. It may be one of a series of workshops, in which case you will need to take the experience of the workshop just finished into the planning of the next ones.

Finishing off

As with the activities at the beginning of the workshop, all of these may not be necessary.

Review deliverables: Review what has been achieved during the day. This is worth doing because it makes the workshop's output explicit. If it was a rocky road to get there or you have not completed all activities, it's even more important to tell everyone what they did.

Review issues and action items: Check whether they are all still relevant. Make sure each one has a participant's name associated with it and, if necessary, a date by which something needs to be done. If someone outside the workshop will actually be taking the action, it still needs to be given to someone inside the workshop so they can pass it on.

Review next steps: Explain what is going to happen with the output from the workshop and if participants can expect a copy of a workshop report. If the workshop has been part of a larger project, it may also be worth explaining how the outputs will fit into the ongoing project.

Evaluate workshop: Sometimes you may want to receive some feedback on how the workshop went.

Workshop owner wrap up: It's appropriate that the owner returns to wrap up the workshop. Hopefully they'll thank participants for their time and input, talk about next steps and if you're lucky, comment on what a tremendous job you've done. Better still, warn them in advance that you'll be doing this so they can prepare themselves.

Documenting the workshop

Most workshops will need to be written up afterwards. This may be part of your role. You'll need to agree the format of this output, preferably before the workshop. There is a range of possible formats:

Photographs of the outputs on the wall. This is simply photographs taken of the outputs which can be emailed to the workshop owner.

A written version of the outputs on the wall. The outputs are typed up with little embellishment as a literal record of what happened in the session, complete with headings and including any notes which were taken by the scribe, if you had one.

A deliverable based on the outputs. The purpose of a workshop if often to provide the input for a particular deliverable such as strategy document, business process and requirements or a plan. In this case, the workshop outputs will be written up more formally. What was effectively a bullet point on a sticky note will be expanded to a full explanation; tables and diagrams will be drawn up. In short, you will be refining raw material into a finished product.

Wider analysis based on the outputs. Similar to the above, this is where the workshop has formed one source of input to a larger process or project. Its outputs will be combined with others to form a finished deliverable.

If the workshop output is going to take much time to document, write up only the action list so that can be sent out as soon as possible.

Follow up on actions

If asked to follow up, it may be because you have become the de facto project manager of work kicked off in the workshop, or because you need the results of those actions to complete your deliverable.

Prepare for the next workshop in the series

If your workshop is one of a series on the same project, you can learn from the one which has just taken place.

If the participants are going to be the same, now you know what they're like and you can plan a workshop to match their expected behaviour. You can also learn from what worked and what did not and build that into the plan for your subsequent workshops. This can be particularly useful if you will be running what is effectively the same workshop but with a different group of people.

Make sure you talk to the owner to gain their input into the planning of the next one. They will also have some thoughts on how the one just completed went and what they would like to see in the next one.

Obtain formal reviews

At the end of workshops, seek feedback on them. You can go to colleagues, the workshop owner or some or all participants. You can simply ask them how it went or provide a questionnaire.

You can also build this kind of feedback into the workshop plan, asking the group if they felt they met the objectives and how effective they thought it was. Here are some sample questions. You would want to amend them for any particular workshop and you may have supplementary questions.

- How clear were the objectives?
- How well did we achieve what we set out to do?
- How well did we use our time?
- How well thought out were our decisions?
- How clear and doable was our action plan?
- How well run was the workshop?
- How well prepared was the facilitator?
- How useful were the supporting materials?

In each case, ask for suggestions for improvement.

Finishing off: Key points

- Review actions and next steps.

- If documentation of the outputs is required, do it as soon as possible.

- Reflect on how the workshop went and learn from it.

11

WHAT NEXT?

If you're already a practising facilitator, you need to keep doing it. If you're new to it, you need to get some practice. If you're new or nervous, you should probably start small or, at the very least, simple and non-controversial.

Networking

Ask other more experienced facilitators for help if you know them. If there are others in your organisation, create an informal network so that you can support each other, discussing problem situations, exchanging ideas for tools and techniques, and reviewing each other's agendas.

Certification

Becoming a certified facilitator, for example through the International Association of Facilitators' (IAF) Certified Professional Facilitator (CPF) programme, will help you to judge your development needs and give you some external feedback on your practice.

It gives you contacts outside your own company and lets you see how facilitation is used by others. It will be proof of your capabilities as a facilitator because you will have been independently assessed by professional facilitators to an international standard.

Training

There are many courses for workshop facilitators. For a course to be effective, if needs to have a high level of practical content. There is nothing like trying it out yourself.

The good news is that many of these skills are about dealing with people, something which, unless you were brought up by squirrels on a desert island, you've been doing your whole life. Often it's about making conscious use of skills you already have.

It is very useful if some of the practical exercises involve people role-playing some of the behaviours facilitators will inevitably have to manage. When I do this, I provide cards containing a short description of the behaviour. A colleague used cards that instructed the holder to be either negative or positive and whether to be active or passive in the way they did so, leaving the precise behaviour up to the individual.

If these mock behaviours are used, instruct the role players to stop doing them once the facilitator has either dealt with them or shown they are unable to do so. Discuss how they were dealt with afterwards as well as strategies that weren't used.

While this approach sounds artificial, I've found that it manages to set up realistic situations for people to deal with. The person making up how a process happens sounds just like someone who doesn't really know how it all works outside their immediate domain. I've found that most people are excellent at acting. They're often channelling people they've come across in real life. I've had a trainee say "Of course you wouldn't get that many things happening in one session," only for another to disagree from their own experience before I needed to.

I end my course with a longer workshop where each trainee takes a section and nobody needs to role play. As it goes on, I use the behaviour cards from the previous exercise to make a pile of situations which have arisen naturally. It's usually at least half of those we pretended to act.

Beyond specific workshop facilitation training, other useful training is around presentation skills, Lean UX, problem solving, negotiation and creativity. Even things such as theatre sports or improvisation will help speed up your thinking and help you to become comfortable working in front of an audience, making connections and dealing with the unexpected.

Record keeping

You may think you'll always remember how you ran a particular workshop. I've certainly found this not to be the case, at least not now that I've run hundreds of them. So keep records of what you did. This mainly means keeping your old agendas so they can be reused. It's also useful to keep track of what happened, what problems came up and how you dealt with them. It can be a lonely job and giving yourself a debrief to reflect on what happened is a useful way to learn from experience. If you're working with colleagues, then you have others to help this process.

Start a library of techniques. These can be sourced from other facilitators, training courses, books and the internet.

Keep a record of rooms which work well for workshops and ones which don't.

Wrap up

The more I think about it, the more I come back to the importance of understanding your objectives and doing sufficient preparation. It gives you the chance to mentally rehearse what could happen and pre-empt problems.

The ultimate measure of success at the end of a workshop isn't how much your plan stood up in practice, nor is it how many interventions you had to perform. It's simply this: did you achieve your objective? If you did, well done. Make sure you reflect on why and how that happened. If you didn't achieve your objective, then reflect on that too. Think also about what you did achieve.

What next: Key points

- Bounce ideas off other facilitators.

- Getting certified helps you to develop.

- Look for training and experience which will broaden your skills.

- Keep records of your workshops for reference and reflection.

- Ask for and listen to feedback.

- Reflect on what happened.

12

AFTERWORD: THE NIGHTMARE

This final section is just for fun. It's a description of a dream I had once about facilitation. I was so amused by it at the time, that I wrote it down immediately, which is why I was able to remember the detail. All I can say is that I hope it is never like this for you.

It was to be a three day workshop in a hotel. We had about 10 minutes to set up and it was due to start at 9.30am. We'd left the workshop kit box in the back of the car at the top of a multi-storey car park and the business analyst I had with me was reluctant to fetch it. We'd also forgotten the brown paper, but we fortunately still had some from a previous workshop, although there was writing on parts of it.

We were still putting it up on the wall when participants started to come in. Coffee had been served and I turned to find that my scribe had rearranged the tables so that although they were in a horseshoe, there were extra tables leading towards me, so it was more like a multi-armed E and people were sitting all over the place.

We set about re-arranging the tables and trying to get rid of the old ones, confusing everyone's drinks in the process. It made things more difficult that the tables had tablecloths and full dinner settings on them and that people sat in completely different places once the tables were in the correct formation. One of the sheets of brown paper slid off the wall.

By this time it was about midday and we hadn't started the workshop yet. I tried to get the customers to sit on the far side of the U so that they would be facing me instead of on both sides. It didn't help that some extra tables had reappeared at various places and some participants, of whom there appeared to be about forty, insisted on sitting at them.

During the general mayhem, as I was about to get everyone to tell me their names and job roles, it became apparent that most had no idea why they were there and some were angry about it. People kept putting up their hands to speak. Not only that, but the system for which we were gathering requirements had already been written. It turned out that this wasn't a requirements gathering session, as I'd been led to believe, but it would be them describing how the system already functioned.

They were just starting to sit in the right places when everyone, including my other staff, rushed out of the room in a game someone had started. It was 12.45 when everyone came crowding back into the room. Lunch was supposed to be at 12.30. We still hadn't begun the workshop.

I was determined to at least find out who everyone was before lunch. There seemed to be more tables than ever by now and the room had increased in size. Everyone had sat in completely different places again.

I introduced myself, saying I would be facilitating for the next two and a half days: I didn't feel like I'd done much so far. I was almost shouting because the room had become so big. Then I asked the person on my far left to introduce themselves. There was no response. I asked again and there was still no response. I thought he must be either deaf, dead or awkward. I was about to ask the person on my far right to begin instead when, mercifully, I woke up.

Appendix 1:
Sample agendas

HOW TO USE THIS SECTION

This section contains a set of example agendas. It is by no means exhaustive and there are not examples in here of every workshop you may need to run. What they show are complete workshop processes which have worked on more than one occasion.

They show how tools and techniques can be built into the process. In some cases, I've provided further ideas of techniques to use.

I have not used the format of agendas I suggest in **The workshop plan** because that would be making them too specific. Instead, I've concentrated on what happens at each stage.

I would be surprised if one of these agendas fits your needs perfectly. When adapting them or building your own, use the guidance on how to plan your workshop process (see the chapter on **The workshop plan**).

For workshops which relate to a particular expertise, if not expert in it yourself, make sure you consult a specialist to help you structure the process e.g. a project manager, test manager, business analyst or designer.

AGENDA LIST

Problem or conflict resolution

A wide range of potential disagreements can be worked through in a workshop. Often, part of a workshop on another theme will require a problem to be resolved. The process below can work well on a small scale as well as for a whole workshop.

When trying to resolve conflict, it is important to make sure the pace is right. Spend time defining the problem and understanding the interests of each party. They need to be clearly brought out so that people, who often haven't been listening to each other, start to listen. That can be half your battle. Sometimes it's all of it.

Define problem

Many arguments happen because people are debating different ideas. Be clear on what the problem is. Sometimes it is also useful to define what the problem is not. Identify examples, if that helps.

Identify positions

If any participants are holding positions on potential solutions, in other words, they already have a solution in mind, these need to be brought out into the open because they will affect the way they discuss solutions and their willingness to be flexible.

Identify interests

Initial positions are often mutually incompatible. What is important are their actual needs, their interests. Once these are identified, it will become clear that the position they hold is just one solution to the problem, but it may not be the best and it may not sit well with other stakeholders. Make sure the interests are worded in such a way that they can become the measures for what would constitute a successful solution.

If possible, the needs can be prioritised. Be clear about why any needs are claimed to be essential. All parties must understand why a particular party sees any need as being essential.

Highlight common needs.

Highlight complementary needs where there is no conflict because meeting that need has no impact on the other party.

Doing this will reduce the size of the problem and enable the parties to find common ground. Focus discussion on what is left. The aim is to make the remainder a common problem for both parties to resolve.

Define options

Come up with as many potential solution options as possible. Deliberately think widely and include any original positions among them.

Discuss options

Discuss each option in the light of the needs identified earlier. Use the needs as criteria by which to review each option. If there are blockers, ask what it would take for the barrier to be removed and explore that possibility.

Keep narrowing the area of debate until everything is agreed or you have gone as far as you can.

Ask what will happen if an agreement is not reached. Compare that to the options that are left.

Other techniques

BATNA

The BATNA is the Best Alternative To a Negotiated Agreement. This is where a party is left if a settlement is not reached. Each one's BATNA is likely to be different. It is useful knowing each one in advance because the one with the better BATNA will be in a stronger negotiating position.

For example, one of my employees tells me that if she doesn't get a pay rise, she'll take up another job offer with the pay she wants. My BATNA is that she leaves and I lose the employee; hers is that she leaves and gets the pay rise. Assuming the roles are equivalent and she's a valued employee, her BATNA is stronger.

One text procedure

The facilitator or another third party listens to the needs of each party and draws up a proposal. This is presented to participants, reviewed and redrafted until no further improvements can be made. At this point, the proposal will either be accepted or the negotiation will need to be abandoned.

Use the past

This technique usually requires some preparation. Look at the ways in which similar issues have been framed by other groups, currently or in history. Ensure lessons are learned from it and look for precedents.

Business scoping

This is for rapid modelling of a whole business or part of a business and then identifying the parts of it which are in scope for a given project. While it can all be documented on flipcharts or stickies, at some point in the workshop, it will be useful to draw it.

Define business purpose

Briefly define what the business does.

Define inputs

What inputs come from outside the business which are processed somehow. From which organisation, business unit, system or people do they originate?

Define outputs

What outputs go out from the business. To which organisation, business unit, system or people do they go?

Define major business functions or systems

What are the major functions or processes within the business? These can be substituted for systems if this is for a systems context.

Match functions to inputs and outputs

To which functions or processes (or systems) do inputs go and from which do outputs come?

Define the scope

Mark which of the above are in scope for the proposed project. If this has been drawn, a line can be marked on the diagram to show the boundary.

Plan project (Example 1)

I believe it's important that the people who will be executing a plan are the ones who put the plan to together. It creates buy-in and transparency, and leads to a higher quality plan because people who knew what they were talking about did the estimates.

Starting point

This approach uses the concept of chunks which constitute small phases. In Agile delivery, these are called iterations, sprints or timeboxes. I will use the term chunk in an attempt to be generic.

Components have been identified, together with their associated requirements. Now they need to be divided into a number of chunks.

Set chunk objectives

Decide how many chunks are likely for this project with approximate dates. Define some objectives for these chunks. This partitioning could be governed by:

- business process;
- process or data affinity;
- technical platform;
- architectural component;
- organisation, i.e. user groups ;
- regular chunk lengths ;
- relationship to an external event during the project.

Assign deliverables to chunks

Divide deliverables amongst the chunks based on the objectives. Give business participants some time to divide them up by moving them around. Suggest criteria to help them such as:

- The rationale for the partitioning above;
- Things that will need to be decided early, such as core functionality or look and feel;

- Complex or contentious deliverables on which work needs to start early;
- Deliverables with known dependencies.

This can be done visually by spreading them out on a wall or large table with each on a piece of paper, card or sticky note.

Review partitioning from technical viewpoint

Having done this, the technical participants become involved. They need to look at the deliverables and see if the groupings make sense from a technical viewpoint. They should review dependencies and components.

Add estimates

Estimates should be added, if they weren't on the original deliverables. If there was no time to do estimates before, the technical participants could have been putting estimates on the deliverables while the business was sorting them.

With the estimates added, how similar are the chunks in size? For agile projects at least, it is often recommended to have them of a regular size to maintain the project's "heartbeat".

Remember to account for any change in the size of the team as the project progresses.

Review chunk contents

Identify the end date of each chunk.

Compare resources available with total deliverables in each chunk. If (or when!) the results don't match, deliverables can then be sorted between chunks if possible.

Some risk planning will need to accompany this work. Some hard decisions may need to be made at this point.

Plan project (Example 2)

In this project, there were four major process areas in scope which were undergoing change, but what was required to make those processes work, from a people, process and technology perspective was not known. Also, there wasn't a common understanding across the whole project team of what was required because it had been run in silos. This workshop resulted in a plan which was understood by each team who came together as a single team.

Check understanding of processes

Make sure all participants understand what the processes are.

Define 'To Do' items

Brainstorm things that need doing based around each stage of the process. Number these actions or deliverables by process so they can be related to parts of the process for risk management.

This will result in an unstructured set of things to do.

Identify risks

Identify risks, then identify actions to mitigate those risks. These can be added to the plan.

Identify action owners

Allocate an owner to each item. If more than one person is named, make duplicates with only one name. This facilitates planning an individual's workload. Write the name in a different colour to the item description.

Estimate

Have each owner provide their own estimate for how long it would take to complete their item. Add this in another colour.

Add deadlines to chunks

Put deadlines on each chunk. Ideally these will be based on actual events or logical milestones. A chunk can be represented by a blank sheet of flipchart paper. The start and end dates can be added on a sticky so they can be changed if required.

Populate chunks

Assign items to each chunk. Estimates should be reviewed for feasibility. For example, part time participants should remember to consider how long other things they do will take so that they don't over-populate a chunk with more than they're capable of delivering.

Move items around as required and revise end dates if necessary.

Plan first chunk in detail

Review its contents, assign dates and meetings. Formally define deliverable and acceptance criteria if it hasn't been done already.

Example output from chunk planning workshop.

Plan project (Example 3)

Brainstorm events

Come up with as many events on a plan as possible without imposing any structure or order.

Order events

Order the events chronologically.

Review events

Work backwards along the timeline, marking dependencies. For each event, ask what needs to happen to reach this point that isn't on the timeline and find out what is already happening.

Risk Management

The project manager will be responsible for the risk register so take their guidance on who should be invited. Make sure it is a range of technical and business stakeholders and try to include at least at least one 'been there, done it' person.

Identify risks

Identify as many risks as possible.

Prioritise risks

Plot the risks on a chart using impact and likelihood. Here is an example chart which could be used. These can be constructed on paper or projected onto a wall. If projected, remember to take a photograph of it so you have a backup record of what was decided.

Impact:	1	2	3	4	5
Probability	Negligible	Minor	Moderate	Significant	Severe
5 Almost certain	Low risk	Moderate risk	High risk	Extreme risk	Extreme risk
4 Likely	Minimum risk	Low risk	Moderate risk	High risk	Extreme risk
3 Possible	Minimum risk	Low risk	Moderate risk	High risk	High risk
2 Unlikely	Minimum risk	Low risk	Low risk	Moderate risk	High risk
1 Rare	Minimum risk	Minimum risk	Low risk	Moderate risk	High risk

Agree how likely each risk is of occurring and what its impact would be. Sometimes this is done as simply High, Medium or Low, but a five point scale is often used such as:

	Likelihood		**Impact**
1.	Rare	1	Negligible
2.	Unlikely	2	Minor
3.	Possible	3	Moderate
4.	Likely	4	Significant
5.	Almost certain	5	Severe

Define actions

Lists of risks can be very long. If they have been prioritised, defining the actions can proceed in priority order to make sure the highest risks are dealt with. Project management can decide at what point it is no longer worthwhile creating an action plan.

Actions can be preventative or mitigating.

Requirements gathering and process modelling

A highly effective way to drive out business requirements is to work through the associated business process. It reduces the chance of gaps in analysis and avoids any assumptions about which parts of the process a future technology solution will cover. This means that the resulting requirements are for an end to end solution. They also tend to run themselves in terms of an agenda because you can simply follow the processes.

Typically these workshops require a cross-section of stakeholders who are the ones performing the business process. These can range from shop floor to executives in some cases and you will need to be prepared for the diversity of working styles.

Define high level processes

Identify the processes which you're going to cover in the workshop. Once you have done this, you will know the volume of work you have to cover. List them on stickies.

Define detail for each process

Choose the main processes first and step through what each one involves, what the steps are, what business rules and requirements there are. List these in stickies of another colour to the higher level process. The first process often takes much longer than the others. This is partly because it may well be the most complicated, but it's also where participants are gaining an understanding of the approach. They will speed up, so bear this in mind when monitoring times of each stage.

Where there is a decision point, do the usual scenario first and come back to alternatives.

The first photograph below shows a simple way of capturing this information. It can be structured properly later in a document. This is easy for customers to follow and quick to record in the workshop. Some of the stickies list the different statuses of an order.

Decision points can be shown by branching into two lines of stickies or even using a square sticky on its side like a diamond to represent standard decision point notation.

The second photograph shows a more complicated way of representing the information by making it into an actual flow chart.

Define data needs

If required, a further iteration could identify data attributes used during the process. Give them their own colour too.

Prioritise

A further pass could add a priority to each sticky or this can be added when the workshop is written up for review later.

Supporting techniques

Prioritisation: Each in turn

Have customer participants mark a priority on each sticky. If supplier participants are also present, they could be providing initial indicative estimates at the same time. Priorities can then be reviewed in the light of the estimates which may lead to a change in priority. It can be time consuming.

Prioritisation: Using preparation

If requirements are known before the workshop, issue the list in advance and have all participants note their own priorities. At the start of the workshop, go through one list. Only those where participants disagree need to be discussed.

Grouping

An area for each priority level can be marked up on the wall and the participants can stand around the wall and group requirements into the four spaces. If anyone disagrees with someone else's, they mark it. Afterwards, discuss the ones people disagreed on.

Using stickies

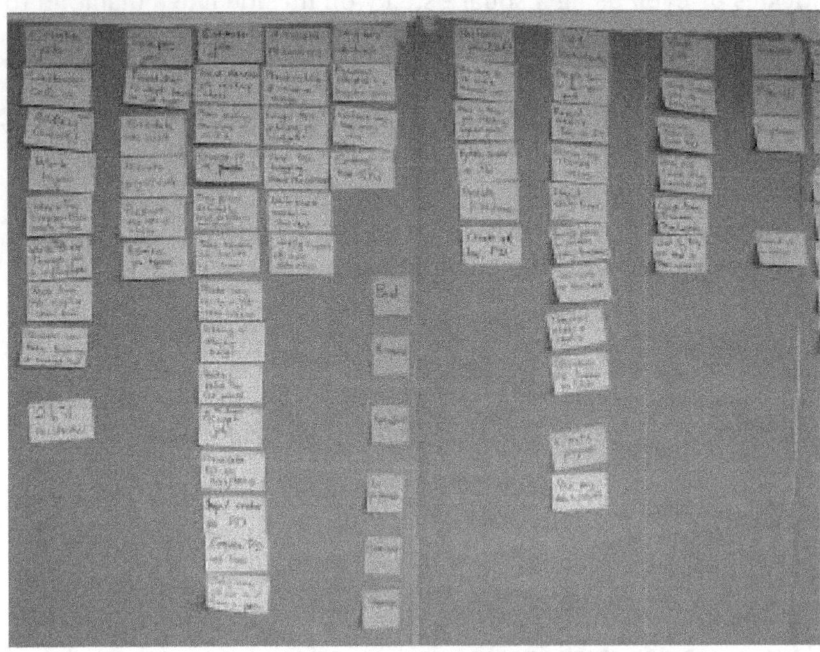

Above: Simple method of capturing processes and requirements using stickies. Below: a more diagrammatic alternative.

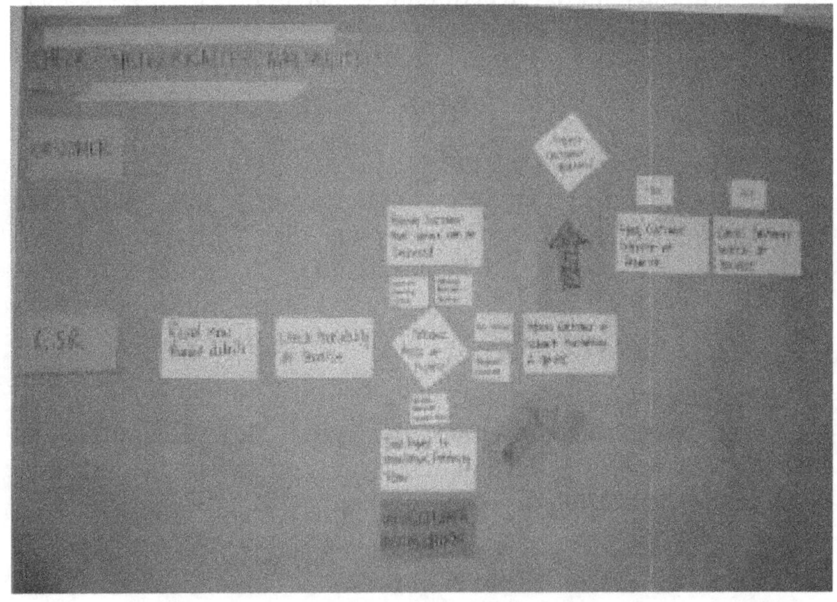

Inputs and outputs

Shows the process at a higher level, but with some context. It flows left to right. New inputs are above and outputs below. Outputs of the previous step can be assumed to be inputs to the next unless marked otherwise e.g. with brackets. You may find this level of detail still requires you to model everything anyway.

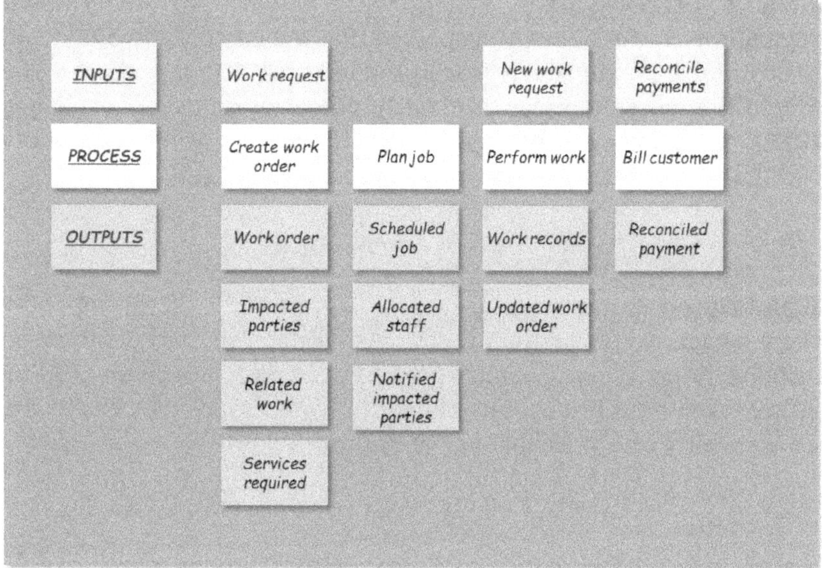

Gaps and redundant practices

Expect to find gaps in the way things are done now. These are often well known and may result in an outpouring of cynicism. Make sure you gather information about them, but be wary of promises of resolving them.

It is not unusual to uncover practices which are no longer required. Use scenarios to test whether they are truly not required. It can be useful to make a note of them being excluded for future reference.

Software package gap analysis

A software package was being introduced to an organisation to support process areas which were subject to government regulation. It was strongly suspected that the customer would want to customise it extensively (rarely a good idea with a package). The aim of the workshop was to identify potential requests for change (RFCs) and shortlist those requiring estimates, as well as to identify configuration requirements (expected for a package).

Process walkthrough

A package consultant uses prepared diagrams to walk through how the package performs the process. As he does so, participants can ask questions. Where changes are required, they are challenged by either consultant or facilitator about how necessary they really are. Those which pass the challenge are noted.

Prioritise

A chart is prepared. Its X-axis represents business benefit with an end zone for essential regulatory requirements. The Y-axis is for effort: with an end zone showing work which would take longer than the date regulation kicked in. These lead to an extreme risk red zone in the top right hand corner.

Business participants map their requirements to the chart in terms of business benefit. Vendor participants move them according to time taken to deliver.

Challenge mapping

A review of the initial mapping of requirements is conducted using questions around:

- Is it regulatory?
- Is there a financial penalty under regulation?
- How many end users would be impacted?
- How many internal departments would be affected if not implemented?

- How many Service Provider companies would be impacted if not implemented?
- What would be the effort impact of not doing it?

Test strategy planning

Agree test types

Agree on the types of testing that need to be done. Ensure all parties have a common understanding of what a particular name means. For example I've seen Business Acceptance Testing, User Acceptance Testing and System Testing used to mean the same thing in different organisations.

If this list has been defined before the workshop, review it within the workshop.

Agree the scope and objectives of each test type. What is this supposed to test? E.g. to ensure business rules are built into the system; to confirm whether response times are acceptable? What risks are these tests aimed at eliminating? This may generate some more test types.

Group test types

Group test types by phase or chunk. A table with chunk by type may be useful.

Determine test environment

This table will give an indication of the technical environment required for this testing.

Check what other environmental requirements there are e.g. what will need to be in place for the testing to happen and who is responsible for planning it.

Determine dependencies

Identify other dependencies for each test type e.g. what needs to be in place, what needs to have been done, what other teams or third parties are involved.

Test data

Determine where test data will come from; who will produce it, where it will be stored and how it will be refreshed.

Acceptance criteria

Define when testers know they have done enough testing; do all bugs identified need to be removed? It is recommended that exit criteria contain measurable overall targets for test coverage and results so that it can be determined whether objectives have been reached and how close the project is to meeting them.

Define responsibilities

This includes who defines tests of different types, who will perform the testing and who is responsible for review and sign off.

Testing process

How will they be done e.g. manually or using a tool, the process for capturing bugs and ensuring they are fixed.

Define testing deliverables

Define any documentation standards and required level of detail or the reports to be used from the tool.

Define tools

Define what tools will be used e.g. for data generation, data version control, running tests.

Actions

Check these have owners, delivery dates and priorities.

Chunk planning

This approach is for planning a piece of a larger project such as a timebox, iteration or sprint. As before, make sure participants are those who will be executing the plan.

Clarify deliverables

Ensure all deliverables for this chunk are visible at the start of the workshop so that the team can see the scope of the planning problem.

Assign deliverables

Assign deliverables, or parts of them, to the appropriate team members. Make sure they have a mix of priorities (that is, that someone doesn't only have Must haves) as contingency is in the lower priority items.

Identify who should be accepting the work as complete. This person could be a business representative or someone from the technical side of the team.

Estimate

Ensure each requirement has an estimate against it. Ideally this will have been made by the person responsible for delivering it. If not, they need to have reviewed it and agreed to it (really agreed, not bullied into agreeing which simply sets them up for failure). Ensure any previously made estimates are reviewed in the light of experience.

Make sure time has been allowed for reviews, meetings and other non-clearly productive time.

Review feasibilty

Check feasibility of the plan. Does each team member have the right amount of work – not too much, not too little? Where there are too many deliverables for the chunk, the business owner or their representative will need to decide which items to drop completely or to move to a later part of the project.

Make calendar plan

Set up a calendar on the wall showing the time period of the chunk. Mark any known dates such as deliverable review meetings. Using stickies will make this flexible.

Plan travel arrangements where this is possible. The earlier this is done, the more likely it is that people will be able to make dates and the lower travel costs will be.

Add any other key dates such as demonstrations, progress meetings etc.

This chart can be left on the team's wall for the duration of the chunk and used as an on-going planning tool.

Identify risks

These are the risks from the main project risk register which are relevant to this chunk. If new ones are identified, ensure they have likelihood, impact and a management plan. Each action should have an owner and may lead to other deliverables.

Deliverable design

It can be used for screens, reports, room layouts, organisational structure, document or presentation. Note that the result will be conceptual and will still require the input of a designer.

Objectives

Initially, state what you are trying to design, its scope and constraints. Define its intended purpose and its acceptance criteria - how you will know when it's achieved its purpose.

Identify requirements and components

Make a list of what needs to appear in the deliverable e.g. fields and buttons; columns and search criteria; chapters, themes; teams and responsibilities. Ideally these can be put onto stickies, if putting up on a wall, or ordinary pieces of paper if the deliverable is being laid out on a table top. Refer back to the purpose to ensure there's a good reason for these being included.

Create deliverable

Items defined in the previous step can be placed on a background.

Business rules, especially for some kind of "IF...ELSE..." structure can be modelled using a flowchart.

Flow charts are also useful for showing navigation around a website where each box is a page.

For screen design, further information can be added to the design as in below.

Whiteboards can be used to draw wireframes, flow charts or other designs.

When obtaining feedback, make sure positive feedback is captured, as well as negative feedback, as this is often forgotten. Apart from it being pleasant to have, it also avoids aspects of the design that were liked being removed in the following iteration of the design.

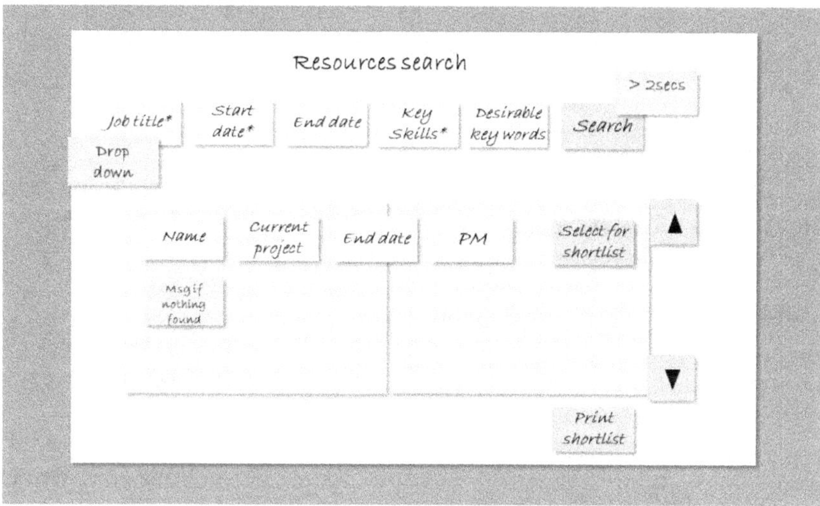

Above: Screen design built using stickies.

Deliverable review

In this instance, a team member has gone off and done some work and is presenting it back to its acceptor for comment.

Clarify deliverable objectives

Begin by re-stating what the deliverable was supposed to show or demonstrate. This helps to ensure it is judged in the right light. E.g.

- If a screen so far shows only examples of data, its layout and format, comments on incomplete validation are not required;
- If a document has been written to show its structure and an indication of content, feedback is not required on formatting issues or the detail of the content.

This will not only help to manage the scope of discussion, but will avoid unwarranted negative opinions about the deliverable. Management of this kind of discussion is the facilitator's job.

Present deliverable

The creator of the deliverable may talk other participants through the piece of work or they may just be given it while the creator notes their reactions. This is particularly useful for testing intuitiveness or understanding.

Review feedback

Summarise the main points of feedback. Ensure action points are given an owner and a completion date. Note any new requirements. Participants may not realise how much new work or rework is being requested as it comes out in conversation, so it is important that this list is made visible and prioritised.

Chunk retrospective

Use at the end of a chunk of work (e.g. a phase, sprint, iteration, timebox) to review the status of deliverables compared to the plan and to learn from how the project is running.

Review previous actions

Start each retrospective by checking to see if all actions from the previous retrospective have been completed and if not, why not. If the team took five actions, but completed none, there's little point taking any more than one action away from this retrospective. Once the team has got better at completing the actions they've committed to then maybe they can increase the amount of actions they take away.

Review deliverables

Team members report progress on their assigned deliverables. Each is either signed off or kept for a future chunk or delivery. This workshop process suits a project approach that focuses on delivery as being success. When I have used this, I've said that "almost complete, I just need to do X" doesn't count as complete. While this was not popular, it did help focus on finishing. Team members really wanted their work considered 'done'. Any new deliverables are identified. Sub-deliverables also need to undergo this process.

A useful way of presenting this information is to have three flipchart sheets, labelled "Signed off", "This chunk" and "Incomplete, not accepted". (I must admit that when I first used this, I'd never heard of a Kanban chart). It shows the result of the review visually and also shows progress though the agenda as deliverables are moved from the central area to one of the other two. I've seen teams spontaneously boo and cheer depending on where each sticky ended up.

Ensure there is one deliverable on each sticky note. An estimate is useful too but need not be there until planning takes place.

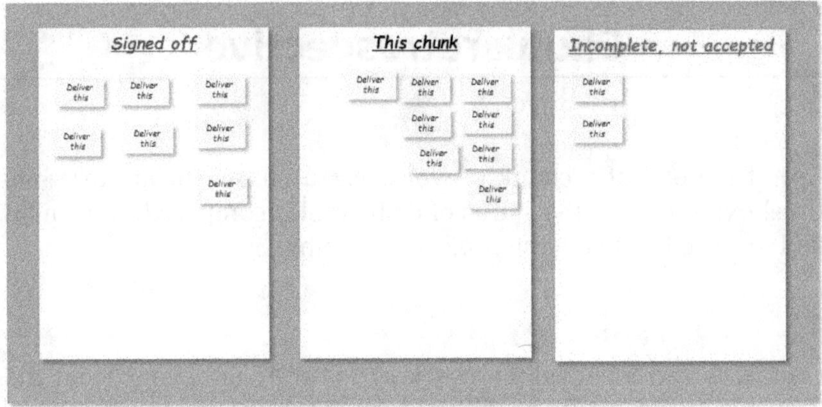

Chunk review

Review estimates

Review how well estimates matched actuals. Make sure any lessons are learned that will help future estimating.

Review project risks

Review how well risks were managed. Note any actions.

Lessons learned

Review the chunk for any other lessons learned, group if necessary and define any actions. Define things in terms of a need, then define a solution to meet it.

Project retrospective

This is a deceptively simple approach. Any project retrospective requires the facilitator to be on the lookout for blame being allocated and individuals accused of mistakes. Without an experienced and neutral facilitator, a retrospective could actually make things worse.

Apart from blame being backward looking, rather than forward looking as this agenda is, it is difficult to blame any single person for anything – despite what politicians or the media try to do. For this reason, a safe environment is vital. There must be no fear of retribution. Emphasise a ground rule about talking from your own perspective, rather than anyone else's.

Ultimately, these should be very positive workshops because they give participants the opportunity to learn and grow.

What went well?

List as bullets. Avoid long discussion, just be clear on what it was. This is particularly necessary on projects which were perceived as failures or at least a difficult journey. The successful aspects are often overlooked. These in themselves can help create a positive mood and it is a useful way to start the workshop.

What needed improving?

List as bullets. Avoid long discussion, just be clear on what it was.

What puzzled you?

List as bullets. Avoid long discussion, just be clear on what it was.

Group

Where any items in the three sets can be clustered, group them so that they can be discussed together.

How to improve

For each item requiring improvement, what needs to happen in the future?

Avoid "Who was responsible for this going wrong?" Concentrate more on "This happened. How do we stop it going wrong again?"

How to keep the good things

For each of the items that went well, understand why it went well and what actions need to be taken to ensure it continues to do so.

Clarify the puzzling

Some of these may have already been resolved, but this section can throw out some interesting findings which have not been captured elsewhere.

For example where someone could have provided better help had they known the purpose of a request.

Supporting techniques

Project timeline

Creating a timeline for the project can be useful to help participants think through the whole project, not just areas that really stuck in their heads. Artefacts from the project can also help stimulate memories.

Graphing your emotions

Have each participant plot their feelings about the project on a graph. Compare them to look for patterns or differences.

Talking stick

If everyone wants to talk at once, use a Talking Stick. The rule is that you can only talk while holding it and you can only hold it a second time on the same topic once everyone else who wants to has had their say.

Better still, make the talking stick a cuddly toy. It will help calm emotions. They may even start stroking it.

Show appreciation

Allow participants to tell each other what they liked about them during the project. This can achieve a certain level of anonymity if it is passed around the room and each person adds to it at least one statement. It's easy to focus on the negatives, but its insistence on the positive is a useful way of achieving balance where relationships have been damaged. It is also a good way of ending the workshop.

Stop, Start, Continue

A simple review technique:

- What should we stop doing?
- What should we start doing that we're not already?
- What should we keep doing?

Postcards

Collect postcards including ones from holiday or those given out free for advertising which you can often find in bars and cafes. Lay them out and ask participants to select a postcard which, depending on the purpose of your workshop, best represents:

- their view of the current situation or indeed any particular topic;
- how they felt the workshop went;
- how they feel the project went.

It is interesting how diverse and creative answers can be. For example after a series of workshops to plan a project, one participant chose a postcard of an airliner. Asked to explain, he said that it was "technically complex, but we're all on board and going in the same direction to the same place."

The technique stimulates in a way that simply asking the question does not.

If I haven't had my pack of postcards with me, I've cut pictures out of newspapers and magazines to use instead.

Checklist

You may wish to use a checklist of areas to prompt ideas e.g.

- Business involvement and empowerment (availability, knowledge, interest, authority);
- Product delivery and accepting deliverables (acceptance criteria, completeness, robustness, estimates);
- Chunking (effectiveness, focus, estimating, prioritisation);
- Roles and responsibilities (clarity, understanding, communication, escalation, empowerment);
- Baselining (configuration management, version control and release management);
- Testing (thoroughness, control, retesting);
- Collaboration and cooperation (contract, teamworking, helpfulness, seamlessness);
- Technology (suitability, capability, complexity, design, estimation, hardware and software integration);
- Project management (ownership, leadership, planning, control change control, attitudes, risk management);
- Resourcing (staff levels, suitability, user involvement);
- Training (trainers, strategy, support, environment, documentation, planning);
- Communication (feedback, communication lines, quality of information);
- Change management (attitudes, strategy, effectiveness, buy-in, sponsorship);
- Support (speed, availability, types, trouble-shooting);
- Data conversion (rules, timing, testing, volatility);
- Testing (strategy, data, tools, sign-off);
- Cutover (timing, strategy, support, hardware and software readiness, contingency planning);
- Administration (hotels and travel, tracking and identifying costs);
- Customer service (relations, disruption of normal service, information).

Speedboat

This is a useful visualisation technique and more interesting way of brainstorming ideas. It's described by Luke Hohmann in his book *Innovation Games*.

Draw a speedboat on the water. This represents the project, deliverable, team, sprint or whatever is the subject of your retrospective. You then get the participants to work on their own, in pairs or teams to come up with anchors; things which are holding back the speedboat. You can make the anchor ropes relative to the size of the problem if you want.

A variation, suggested by Marc Loeffler, is to make it a sailing boat and, as well of, or even instead of the anchors, stick up participants' ideas as the gusts of wind which will blow the boat across the water. This gets participants thinking positively.

Obviously you still need to explore each idea, or prioritise the ones to talk about.

Organisation strategy

An internal service provider wanted to offer its services to the wider market. In order to do that, it needed a clear strategy. This had only ever been talked about before, but never properly described.

Define vision and drivers

What is the business vision and why?

Define design criteria

These were criteria which would underlie the future business. For example, they would only offer services they already provided to their parent organisation; staff levels would match normal demand with sub-contractors being used to manage exceptional peaks or specialisms; work would be recorded to identify its true cost.

Define proposed services

The services the company is intending to offer the market. Some of these may be new. The scope of activities involved in these services is described.

State skillset source in the organisation

For each service, the parts of the organisation where this skillset exist is listed, including from the parent company or any gaps.

Identify differentiators

Participants are challenged to come up with how their organisation could differentiate itself from the competition.

Define timescale

The timescale for delivery of this service.

Organisation business planning

This agenda looks at an organisation's plans for the coming year. It could be a team within a wider organisation or the whole company.

Current state review

List what can be learned from the previous year.

Present on where the work came from by customer, segment, channel or whatever makes sense.

Define any expectations for the coming year, including any planned growth areas.

Define products and services

List existing products and services. Add any potential new ones.

Define products and services

If existing products and services are well understood, this could be limited to the new ideas.

Provide an overview of each product or service defining it and listing its key elements. Explain its value to the client, including what issues it would address and list any potential clients.

How much was there and is there

Picking up on the initial overview:

- Present on what work was done in the previous year and what is in the pipeline for the coming year;
- Define customers, segments and regions.

Capability

Review the organisation's capability.

- What are the areas of expertise?
- Who are the experts, how many are there and how are they supported?

- Is there any succession planning in place?

Identify team strengths and gaps.

Partnerships

Identify any potential internal or external partners and their role in a partnership.

If supporting the products and services of a larger organisation, discuss how capability and offerings could be wrapped around them to add value. Come up with new market areas and target and discuss how value could be added. Identify any opportunities and actions to be taken.

Review actions

Given what has been said during the workshop, identify any remaining actions e.g. staff numbers, training, ways of working, technology, sales and marketing.

Partnering propositions

I ran a number of workshops where one company was looking to partner with another because they felt they had complimentary products and services. In each case, participants were tasked with doing some thinking or some research before the workshop as to some opportunities they saw in the market. This agenda could be adapted to an organisation seeking new propositions internally as well.

Organisation overviews

Each company gives an informal talk on their respective strategy, brand, capabilities, company direction and perception issues. A market analyst or similar could also invited to provide an external view. There is opportunity to discuss and clarify. External analyst would provide context.

In my workshops, presentation software was not allowed, although they could use a whiteboard. This was to ensure the presentation was fresh and avoid standard packs of slides. The facilitator took notes of the presentation visibly on a flipchart.

Opportunity presentations

Each participant was given a few minutes to describe opportunities they saw in the market, explaining their reasoning.

Ideas were then grouped and named.

Define propositions

Participants divide themselves into groups and work their way through propositions of interest to them. They have to:

- Define the proposition and flesh it out;
- Define the business problem it aims to address;
- List some potential customers.

Present propositions

Each group present their propositions to the rest of the group. There is discussion. Amend any propositions as a result of this discussion.

Prioritise ideas

Prioritise propositions using a 2x2 matrix. The axes of the grid are:

- Relationship to joint strengths;
- Market need.

Next steps

Pull together the actions and build a plan based on the highest priority propositions.

Align IT and business strategy

An IT strategy had been developed by an organisation, but it made little sense to the business because their business needs had not been formally documented and the relevance of the initiatives had not been shown. As a result, there was no buy-in from the business around the technology initiatives.

Business aims

Briefly list these along with what is driving them.

Identify challenges

List current challenges faced by the company.

Identify needs to overcome challenges

Alongside each challenge, list what is needed to overcome them.

Identify barriers to meeting the needs

There are reasons why these have not already been dealt with. List barriers alongside them.

Identify actions to overcome the barriers

The actions required to overcome the barriers are then listed, together with owners and dates.

Describe initiatives

With all that context, the initiatives are prioritised by business benefit and ease of implementation.

Map initiatives to business needs

This mapping was what brought together what IT had already come up with to show what its purpose was.

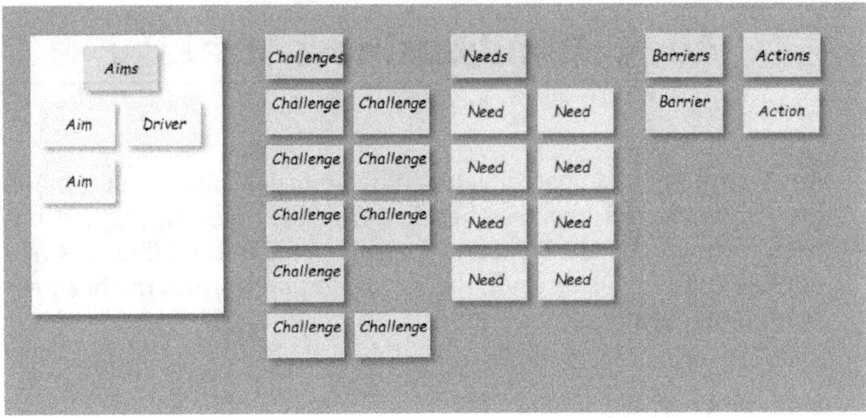

Aims
Aim
Driver
Aim
Challenges
Challenge
Challenge
Challenge
Challenge
Challenge
Challenge
Challenge
Challenge
Needs
Need
Need
Need
Need
Need
Need
Need
Need
Barriers
Barrier
Actions
Action

Design a team building event

Brainstorm ideas

Come up with as many ideas as you can for the event. Encourage broad and creative thinking.

Define event purpose

Confirm the purpose of the event. Why is it being held? What is it supposed to achieve? This will identify the requirements for the event. Define ways of that the success of the event will be measured.

Filter ideas through the requirements

Review each idea in the light of the purpose and measures. Discard any that do not match sufficiently. There is no reason why ideas cannot be combined.

Identify risks to success

You will be left with a much shorter list of ideas. Looking at risks is not only good planning, but could help reduce the list further if required. Look at what risks there are on each idea, how likely they are to happen and how great the impact would be if they did (e.g. someone being injured, someone refusing or unable to participate) and what plans can be put in place to overcome them.

Detailed planning

Having selected an idea for the event, it needs to be planned. Break it down into component parts such as permissions, budget, bookings, travel, catering. Identify dependencies and owners of actions.

Improve something

Perform a SWOT

Take whatever it is, for example a team, a product, a service, an idea and perform a SWOT analysis on it.

- What strengths does it have? What is it good at? How is it most effective? What is valued about it?
- What weaknesses does it have? Where are the gaps in capability?
- What opportunities are there for it? What is untapped in its use?
- What threats are there to it? What could happen to damage it or make it redundant?
- It may be also worth identifying any constraints, perceived or real.

Analyse the SWOT

- How do we maintain the strengths or make them stronger?
- How do we address the weaknesses?
- How do we take advantage of the opportunities?
- How do we overcome the threats?
- Review the constraints. Why are they there? Are they necessary? Is there a way around them?

Create action plan

Take the actions and prioritise them by benefit and effort to implement.

With that information, build them into a plan with dates and owners.

Design a training course

Define objectives

Define what the course is supposed to achieve, its learning objectives.

Brainstorm topics

What will it need to cover to meet those objectives?

Identify main messages for topics

How could you sum up the learning message for each topic? Try to have no more than three messages for each topic.

Define topic content

For each topic, think of ways of getting those messages across. Identify whether they are information heavy or skills based. Come up with some different ways of delivering that learning. Come up with a number of options ranging from how it's always done to something that is daring or outlandish.

Improve staff engagement

Analyse staff engagement

Ask what is working, what is not working and what is missing. This is effectively a Stop, Start, Continue exercise. Come up with as many as you can.

Group results

Where possible, group the results. If any of different type are in the same group e.g. a stop and a start, what does that tell you?

Identify causes

- For problems, what are their causes, why is it like this?
- For successes, what are their causes, why is it like this?
- For new ideas, why have they not been introduced before?

Identify potential actions

Come up with actions and solutions.

Prioritise actions

Prioritise the actions and solutions to decide how effective each would be and how difficult it would be to implement.

Create action plan

Put together an action plan, being careful to include any implied actions which have not yet been explicitly stated. Ensure each has an owner and a date and that any dependencies with other actions is identified.

Appendix II: Templates and checklists

Preparation checklist

1. There is an involved owner or their empowered delegate.
2. The objective is measurable.
3. Deliverables have been defined.
4. Participants are suitably empowered and knowledgeable.
5. There will be a note taker, if required.
6. The room is large enough for the number of participants in the layout required.
7. There is space in the room to display the outputs from the workshop as they are created.
8. The room has any services required such as power points, wireless connection.
9. Breakout rooms have been booked if required.
10. The facilitator will have access to the room before the workshop starts in order to set up.
11. Parking and access to the room has been arranged for facilitator and participants.
12. Catering has been arranged.
13. An informative invitation or briefing has been sent.
14. Name badges have been prepared.
15. Reception has been notified of any visitors, if required.
16. Pens, stickies, scissors, whiteboards, flipcharts, stands and brown paper etc have been arranged.
17. Any handouts have been prepared.
18. Any pre-reading for participants has been prepared and issued.

Workshop plan checklist

1. There are interim deliverables.
2. Each stage has a time estimate.
3. Physical outputs from each stage link to each other where required.
4. Attendees will be ready to participate in each stage of the discussion.
5. A seating plan has been created, if required.
6. The plan takes account of known participant availability.
7. The plan has been documented.
8. The plan has been reviewed by the workshop owner and any co-facilitators.
9. The more thorough the plan, the more smoothly the workshop will run.

Workshop plan

This is the workshop plan format from earlier in the book. You may not always need this much detail, but it helps me make sure my approach works. I usually put mine in a table.

Stage of the process	A short title explaining what this part of the workshop is about.
Process	Break down that stage of the workshop into the steps you're going to follow. Include how you will deal with this physically and any tools or techniques you'll use, including whether this will be full group or breakout group. Remember to include any comfort or meal breaks.
Deliverable	Identify the output of each stage of the workshop.
Time taken	Define how much time you're going to allow for each step.
Completion time	By writing down the time when I estimate this part of the workshop will be finished, I give myself a quick reference guide to how well I'm tracking during the workshop and it keeps me aware of my deadline. If I meet my interim deadlines, chances are I'll meet my final one of the end of the workshop.

Workshop log

Here's an example of what you may want to capture, or the reflection you may want to stimulate, after a workshop.

Title   A name for the workshop.

Date

Type   e.g. Business Requirements / Strategy / Departmental design / Planning / Prototype review / Roles and responsibilities definition / Retrospective etc

Customer   Who was the customer for this workshop?

Duration   E.g. 1 day

Attendees   Could include facilitators, participant names, their roles or at least how many there were.

Objective   Include any priority or interdependency.

Inputs   Any documents, previous workshops

Deliverables   What were the outputs?

Preparation   What problems came up, how did you deal with them? How would you deal with them next time?

Process review How did you go about reaching the objective? What was the process? What tools and techniques did you use at each stage? How long did it take? How did the agenda go? Would there have been a better way of reaching the objective? Did any exercises fall flat? Why? How did your planned agenda compare with reality?

What problems came up, how did you deal with them? How would you deal with them next time?

What went well? Why

Planned process	What you had planned to do in the workshop.
Actual process	What actually happened in terms of the order of activities and what those activities were.
Feedback	Were there any comments from participants?

Workshop review questions

These are some suggested questions which could be put on a feedback form. You could create a standard form for yourself or change it to suit a particular workshop or area on which you're looking for feedback.

Workshop title and date
Customer name and company

Score the following on a range e.g. 1 - 5. Allow space for comments.

The workshop:

- Use of the agenda to structure discussion
- The results of the workshop
- Any reports produced by the facilitator after the workshop

The facilitator's ability:

- Preparing objectives and agenda
- Adaptability
- Handling of workshop participants
- Keeping the group's focus and direction on track
- Explaining the process so you knew what was happening
- Enabling you to freely contribute your thoughts and opinions

Open questions

Describe any benefits from the workshop process.
Describe any problems caused by using the workshop process.
Did the process the workshop followed meet the objectives stated? If not, why not?
Was the pace right? Or was it too fast / too slow?

Do you consider the time spent by your staff was a good
investment?
How can we improve future workshops?
Would you use this facilitation service again?
May we publicise your comments in promotional literature?
May we use your company or name as a reference?

ABOUT THE AUTHOR

Kevin Barron has worked in industry and consulting for more than 25 years and has been running workshops for at least 20 of those. He has led teams, worked on projects and delivered training across many sectors including banking, media, retail, wealth management, telecommunications, transport, IT services, utilities, local and national government, and manufacturing. He has facilitated hundreds of workshops in the UK, Australia, New Zealand, Sweden and Germany. He is also an experienced business analyst and agile practitioner.

Find out more about KA Barron at www.kabarron.com You can also connect with him on Twitter at @kabarronauthor, on Facebook at www.facebook.com/kabarronbooks and if you feel like it, send him an email at kevin@kabarron.com.

ALSO BY KEVIN BARRON

Kevin Barron writes in other genres too. Here are some more of his books.

Travel and humour

Into the blue

Half-planned travels of an amateur vagabond

Kevin Barron feels guilty if he stays at home and does nothing. His solution is to visit other countries and do nothing there instead. An added benefit is that writing about it gives him something to do at home.

Lose your ticket before you've even set off, find out what whalers think of Greenpeace, dodge dive-bombers, meet dangerous truckers, interview a tennis star, witness horror, walk all night, fish for your dinner, watch sunsets in the wilderness, ride legendary highways, stargaze in the Rockies, hitch-hike through the outback, be rescued by an angel, become Robin Hood, escape from Colditz.

This collection of stories covers more than a decade of travel, so throw your backpack over your shoulder and head off...into the blue.

Not there yet

Wandering home with an amateur vagabond

When you leave, at what point do you start going home? And when you leave and don't come back, where is home?

Moving to another country for a while provides an excellent opportunity to travel on the way. Having threatened The Big Trip for years, Kevin Barron finally takes the plunge and, as a result, finds that the idea of home is not as clear as it used to be.

Kayak in the rain, meet an Aboriginal elder, make conversation with a grumpy barber, kill sheep, crash a car, eat entrails, be in the Middle East on 9/11, ride legendary highways, find yourself face to face with an elk, get lost in the African night, have the best view at Shangri-La, fight a fire, be ill on an overnight bus, search for intruders, flirt, haggle, dance, joke, eat, hike, misunderstand, leave home and return.

This collection of stories follows those of Into the blue, so throw your backpack over your shoulder again and set off on the never ending journey home.

Tales of Socks and Splendour

The Grumpete is a disgusting yet warm hearted character who lives alone in a land beyond the Ocean of Spleg. Embarking on an adventure one day, he encounters the Kazza Princess in a distant castle and their lives are never the same again.

Join the foul-bummed Grumpete and the kimmering Kazz as they shine, explode, wander, flatulate, burn, run, reproduce, eat and fight their way through a series of far-fetched adventures in glorious nonsense verse.

Whether read out loud or quietly to yourself where no one will find you, these fast-moving and humorous poems are sure to entertain children of all ages...apart from perhaps those of a delicate disposition.

Adventure novels (as KA Barron)

Light Funnel

The first volume of the Light Funnel series

A father in despair. An ancient destiny. A darkness that can change everything.

Fear has kept ancient enemies apart for centuries, but the Archbishop has made a discovery which will overturn the balance of power.

Falling between worlds, young Charlie Denham and his father Richard find themselves on opposite sides when war looms. The descendants of lost crusaders now face a decisive conflict with the Delf who wield demons of fire.

As darkness pours from the earth and armies gather, Richard and Charlie will face the nightmare from a lost past which threatens to consume both worlds. They must find each other, and escape the approaching storm, if they are to have any hope of staying alive or returning home again.

Light Needle

The second volume of the Light Funnel series

In dreams, something is stirring.

Eight years have passed since the events described in Light Funnel. An uneasy peace has existed between the Order and the Delf. Now, rumblings of dissent threaten a return to war.

Inspired by dreams, Jack Silver searches for the descendants of the adventurers who left Outreterre centuries before and never returned. With their help, the Delf could be overthrown forever.

Former adversaries Berwick, Rodon and Raul secretly follow Silver and his protectors across the sea; Solimo, still haunted by his experiences, is about to face his greatest fear, while a footloose Charlie Denham will soon be fleeing for his life from forces he does not understand.

For an old enemy has found a way out of Limbo and will stop at nothing to purge the worlds.

When he returns, a great city will burn and a society will be torn apart. Only a fragile web of alliances, old and new, stands before the terrible new power emerging from Limbo.

In this second book in the Light Funnel series, multiple storylines weave together culminating in a climactic confrontation.

Later books in the series will be:
Light Cradle
Light Mage